"유엔사령부"의 실체와 그 문제점
Real Identity of the "United Nations Command"(UNC) and Its Problems

"유엔사령부"의 실체와 그 문제점
Real Identity of the "United Nations Command"(UNC) and Its Problems

초판 1쇄 발행 2021년 10월 12일

지은이	가짜 '유엔사' 해체를 위한 국제캠페인
펴낸곳	도서출판 4.27시대
주소	서울시 종로구 통일로 162 덕산빌딩 502호(교남동)
전화	02-735-4270
팩스	02-735-4271
이메일	427era@gmail.com

ISBN 979-11-971106-8-9 03300

값 15,000원

Published by
International Campaign to Abolish the Fake 'UNC'
(www.fakeunc.org)

Copyright © 2021 by International Campaign to Abolish the Fake 'UNC'
All rights reserved.

First English Edition 2021

Printed in Seoul, Korea

가짜 "유엔사" 해체 자료집 2 · Pamphlet No. 2 on "UNC"

"유엔사령부"의 실체와 그 문제점
Real Identity of the "United Nations Command"(UNC) and Its Problems

가짜 '유엔사' 해체를 위한 국제캠페인

도서출판 4.27시대

차례

part 1 "유엔사령부"의 실체와 그 문제점   7

머리말   9

I   "유엔사"는 유엔의 전문기구나 보조기구가 아니다   13
     1. 1950년 6월 25일 안보리결의 82호의 문제점   14
     2. 1950년 6월 27일 안보리결의 83호의 문제점   20
     3. 1950년 7월 7일 안보리결의 84호의 문제점   23

II   "유엔사"는 한국 주권을 침해했다   41
     1. 미국 통제 하 한국군의 예속   41
     2. 북한 침략과 점령   45
     3. 남북 평화와 발전의 방해   52

III   "유엔사"는 미국법을 위반하여 창설되었다   55
     1. 유엔참여법 위반   55
     2. 미국 헌법 위반   57

IV   "유엔사"는 일본 평화헌법을 위반했다   61
     1. 헌법 9조 '전쟁능력' 금지의 위반   61
     2. 일본의 한국전쟁 참전   63
     3. 허위 '유엔-일본정부 간 SOFA' 설정과 "유엔사" 병참기지화   66

V   "유엔사" 해체는 오래 지연되었다   69
     1. 유엔은 이미 "유엔사" 해체를 요청했다   69
     2. "유엔사"는 1978년부터 허울뿐인 집단이다   72
     3. 퇴물이 된 "유엔사" 재활성화 시도   73
     4. 한국전쟁의 지속을 위한 "유엔사" 명칭 사용   76

VI   결론   79

부록A — 가짜 "유엔사령부" 해체를 위한 선언서   84
부록B — 실행위원회   86
부록C — 지지단체와 개인들   87

part 2　Real Identity of the "United Nations Command" (UNC) and Its Problems　93

Foreword　95

I　"UNC" is Not a Specialized Agency or Subsidiary Organ of the UN　99
    1. Problems in the Security Council Resolution 82 of June 25, 1950　100
    2. Problems in the Security Council Resolution 83 of June 27, 1950　106
    3. Problems in the Security Council Resolution 84 of July 7, 1950　108

II　"UNC" Has Violated Sovereignty of Korea　125
    1. Subjugation of South Korean Military under U.S. Control　125
    2. Invasion and Occupation of North Korea　129
    3. Obstruction of South-North Cooperation Projects　136

III　"UNC" Was Created in Violation of U.S. Laws　139
    1. Violation of the "UN Participation Act"　139
    2. Violation of the U.S. Constitution　141

IV　"UNC" Has Violated Japan's Peace Constitution　145
    1. Violation of Article 9's Prohibition against "War Potential"　145
    2. Japan's Participation in the Korean War　147
    3. Creation of Bogus "UN-GOJ SOFA" and "UNC" Logistic Bases　150

V　Dissolution of "UNC" Is Long Overdue　153
    1. UN Already Called for Dissolution of "UNC"　153
    2. "UNC" Has Been a Hollow Outfit from 1978　156
    3. Trying to Revitalize the Obsolete "UNC"　157
    4. Use of "UNC" to Continue the Korean War　160

VI　Conclusion　163

Appendix A—Declaration for Dissolution of the Fake "UN Command"　168
Appendix B—Steering Committee　171
Appendix C—Supporting Organizations and Individuals　172

part 1
"유엔사령부"의 실체와 그 문제점

머리말

2020년 우리는 공식적으로 끝난 적이 없는 가장 긴 전쟁 중 하나인 한국전쟁 발발 70주년을 기념했습니다. 이 역사적인 기념일과 동시에 1950년 7월에 소위 "유엔사령부"(UNC)가 창설된 지 70주년이 되는 해이기도 합니다. 지난 70년 동안 한국전쟁을 다룬 많은 책들이 출간되었습니다. 불행히도 이 책들 대부분은 "유엔사"의 실체와 역할에 대해 거의 관심을 기울이지 않습니다.

이것은 유엔 기구입니까, 아닙니까? 유엔기구가 아니라면 누가, 왜 만들었습니까? 이 수상한 기구의 임무는 무엇이며, 그것이 오늘날에도 한국에 존재하는 이유는 무엇입니까? 이 기구가 평화를 유지하기 위해서 한국에 있는 겁니까, 아니면 남북화해와 교류를 막기 위해 있는 겁니까? 그 답은 이 기구가 2018년부터 남북 협력사업을 막는 조치를 취했을 때 명확해졌습니다.

한국전쟁을 영구히 종식시키고 한반도의 평화통일을 이루기 위해서는 가능한 한 빨리 한국과 일본에서 미국의 "유엔사"를 해체해야 합니다. 그러기 위해 미국과 일본과 한국 민중의 노력이 절박하다고 믿습니다. 그럼 우리는 어떻게 해야 할까요?

우리는 이 목표를 실현하기 위한 첫 번째 단계가 유엔의 직접 통제 하에 있지 않은 이 이상하고 전능한 "유엔사"의 실제 역사와 정체성에 대해 스스로 교육하는 것이라고 믿습니다. 매우 안타까운 일이지만 오늘날 한국에 있는 대다수의 사람들은 여전히 "유엔사"가 한국전쟁 초기에 유엔에 의해 설립된 유엔의 군사기구라고 믿고 있을지도 모릅니다. 우리는 이 이야기가 사실이 아니라는 것을 이 책자에서 보여주고자 합니다.

이 책자에서 다루게 될 다른 문제로는 "유엔사" 설립 시기, 군사기구로서의 법적 근거, 그 임무와 역할의 변질과정, 그리고 한국, 일본, 미국, 유엔 등에 끼친 부정적인 영향 등이 포함됩니다.

이들 질문에 대한 답변은 유엔, 미국, 한국, 일본의 역사적 문서와 다양한 서적, 기사 및 뉴스 보도를 기반으로 합니다.

사실 "유엔사"의 숨은 역사를 찾기가 쉽지는 않았지만 불가능한 것도 아니었습니다. 진실을 찾는 중에, 우리는 미국 관리들이 유엔의 이름 아래 유엔과 한국전쟁에 관해 어떻게 세계를 속이려고 했는가를 보여주는 충격적인 증거를 발견했습니다. "유엔사" 신화는 1950년 한국전쟁 발발부터 시작된 미국의 선전전에서 확실히 중요한 역할을 해왔습니다. "유엔사"는 "합법적 유엔기구"도 아니고 오랜 역사를 가진 유엔 헌장 제7장 "집단안보 조치"도 아닙니다. 과거에 "유엔사"가 한국에서 한 일은 유엔의 "경찰조치"도 아니었습니다. 게다가 "유엔사"의 외국군대는 UN헌장 제43조의 "유엔군"이 아니었습니다. 사실 그들은 미국 주도의 다국적군에 불과했습니다.

"유엔사"에 대한 모든 오해를 파헤치고 최종적으로 폐기해야 할 때입니다. 그것이 오래된 신화와 거짓말에서 벗어나는 가장 좋은 방법입니다.

이는 한국과 일본 국민이 "유엔사"의 족쇄로부터 국가주권을 되찾고자 할 때 중요합니다. 특히 "유엔사"의 활동이 남한에서 계속 허용되는 한 한국 정부가 미군으로부터 전시작전통제권을 되찾으려는 노력은 헛수고가 될 것입니다. 결국 "유엔사"는 단지 미군과 워싱턴 관리들에 의해 통제되고 있는 또 다른 미국의 군사도구일 뿐입니다.

세계인들이 이 진실을 정확히 이해할 때, 국제사회는 미국정부에 "유엔사"를 부활시키는 대신 해체하라고 강력히 요구할 수 있습니다. 우리는 이 책자를 통해 더 많은 사람들이 "유엔사"의 실체와 어두운 역사를 이해하고 가짜 "유엔사"의 즉각적 해체를 위한 국제적 요구에 동참할 수 있기를 바랍니다. "유엔사" 해체는 지난 70년 동안의 유엔헌장 정신의 유린을 종식시킴으로써 한국, 일본, 미국 국민의 이익뿐만 아니라 유엔의 목표와 원칙 회복에도 기여하게 될 것입니다.

이장희 교수
가짜 "유엔사" 해체를 위한 국제캠페인
실행위원장

2021년 9월 8일, 서울

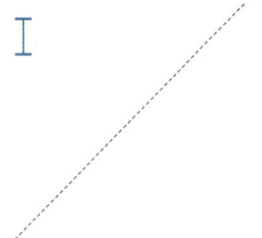

"유엔사"는 유엔의 전문기구나 보조기구가 아니다

미국 정부는 일반적으로 유엔안전보장이사회 결의 82호(1950년 6월 25일), 결의 83호(1950년 6월 27일) 및 결의 84호(1950년 7월 7일)에 따라 미국 주도의 "유엔사령부"가 설립되었다고 주장합니다. 이에 더하여 또한 미국 정부는 1950년 평화와 안전의 회복을 위한 유엔의 "경찰조치"를 위해 "유엔군"의 일원으로 한국에 군대를 파견했다고 주장해왔습니다. 이러한 선전은 국제사회뿐만 아니라 많은 미국인과 한국인들이 소위 "유엔사령부"가 유엔의 전문기구 또는 보조기구로 설립되었다고 믿도록 만들었습니다.

그러나 이러한 주장은 매우 심각한 오해의 소지가 있습니다. 예를 들어, 현재 "유엔사" 웹사이트에는 "북한의 남침에 따라 1950년 7월 24일 유엔사(UNC)가 창설됐다"고 주장하고 있습니다. 또한 "우리가 알고 있는 유엔사령부는 통합사령부"라고 말하고 있습니다.[1]

그러나 누가 "유엔사"를 만들었는지에 대해서는 침묵하고 있습니다. 진실은 무엇입니까? "유엔사"의 실체와 문제점을 파악하기 위해서는 1950년 6월 25일(한국 시간) 한반도에서 무력충돌이 발발한 직후 유엔안보리 결의 82, 83, 84호가 어떻게 채택되었는지 유심히 살펴볼 필요가 있습니

---

[1] www.unc.mil, "About" 참조

다. 유엔헌장에 따라 채택되었는지, 결의안이 언급한 내용은 정당한지, 결의가 충실히 이행되었는지 여부에 대해서 말입니다.

1. 1950년 6월 25일 안보리결의 82호의 문제점

유엔헌장 제24조에 따르면, 안전보장이사회는 "국제평화와 안보 유지에 대한 일차적 책임"을 가지고 있습니다. 헌장 제7장은 "평화에 대한 위협, 평화의 파괴, 침략행위"가 존재하는 상황에 대처할 때 안전보장이사회의 구체적인 절차와 권한을 제시합니다.

헌장 제39조는 특히 안전보장이사회가 1) 위에서 언급한 평화에 대한 위협, 평화의 파괴, 침략행위의 "존재를 결정"한 다음, 2) "국제평화와 안보를 유지하거나 회복하기 위하여 권고를 하거나 아니면 헌장 제41조와 제42조에 따라 취해야 할 조치를 결정하도록" 요구합니다.

1950년 6월 25일(미국 동부시간) 안보리는 미국 정부의 요청에 따라 한국에서 발생한 무력충돌에 대해 논의하기 위한 첫 회의를 열었습니다. 유엔사무총장에게 보내는 메시지에서 유엔주재 미대표부 부대표는 주한 미대사의 전신에 따라 "북한군이 6월 25일 이른 아침(한국 시간) 여러 지점에서 대한민국 영토를 침공했다"고 단순히 주장했습니다. 그리고는 미국 대표가 북한이 "평화의 파괴와 침략행위"를 저질렀다고 비난했습니다.[2] 안보리는 비슷한 주장을 하는 서울의 유엔한국위원회 전신도 참고했습니다.

"한국 정부는 6월 25일 오전 4시경 북한군이 38선을 따라 강력한 공격을 시작했다고 밝혔습니다."

---

2 S/1495. S는 안보리를, 1495는 안보리공식문서의 일련번호를 의미합니다.

그러나 이 전신에는 북한에서 방송된 다른 이야기도 포함되어 있었습니다.

> "평양라디오의 13시 35분 주장 : 남한이 밤에 선을 넘어 침공한 것에 대해…인민군이 단호한 반격으로 침략군을 격퇴하도록 지시했다…"[3]

따라서 6월 25일 발생한 무력충돌의 기원에 대한 분쟁이 있었던 것은 분명합니다. 이런 상황에서 안보리는 양국 정부대표를 안보리회의에 초청하여 분쟁에 대한 공정한 청문회를 개최할 책임이 있습니다. 유엔헌장 제32조는 다음과 같이 명시하고 있습니다.

> "유엔회원국이 아닌 국가는 안전보장이사회에서 고려 중인 분쟁의 당사자인 경우 분쟁과 관련된 토론에 투표권 없이 참여하도록 초대되어야 한다."

비록 미 유엔대사는 6월 25일 안보리회의에 주미 한국대사 장면(John M. Chang)을 초청하고 장면 대사는 한국정부의 주장을 다시 반복하며 유엔의 신속한 조치를 촉구했지만, 안보리는 북한정부 대표의 회의 참석을 위한 초청은 하지 않기로 결정했습니다.

상대국의 의견을 직접 듣기 위해 당시 안보리회원국이었던 유고슬라비아대표(Mr. Bebler)는 "북한정부가 안보리에 참석해 정부의 입장을 설명하도록" 초청하는 결의안을 제출했습니다.[4] 그러나 이 결의안은 3개 안보리 회원국(이집트, 인도, 노르웨이)이 기권하고 소련과 중공(대만 장개석 대표가 여전히 자리를 차지하고 있었음)이 부재한 상태에서, 미국과 미국 동맹 5개국의 반대로 채택되지 않았습니다.

만약 유고슬라비아의 결의안이 채택되었다면 북한군이 남한 진격을 중지했을 지 누가 알겠습니까? 성급히 판단하느라 안보리는 남한 관리들의

---

[3] S/1496
[4] S/1500

주장만 따라 북한이 '평화의 파괴'에 대한 책임이 있다고 결정하는 미국의 일방적 결의안5을 채택하고 말았습니다. 그렇게 함으로써 안보리는 유엔헌장에 따른 조치의 공정성과 합법성에 대해 많은 의구심을 불러 일으켰습니다. (참고.1, SCR82,6 S/1501, 1950.6.25.)

UNITED NATIONS
SECURITY
COUNCIL

GENERAL
S/1501
25 June 1950
ORIGINAL: ENGLISH

RESOLUTION CONCERNING THE COMPLAINT OF AGGRESSION UPON THE REPUBLIC OF KOREA ADOPTED AT THE 473RD MEETING OF THE SECURITY COUNCIL ON 25 JUNE 1950

The Security Council

Recalling the finding of the General Assembly in its resolution of 21 October 1949 that the Government of the Republic of Korea is a lawfully established government "having effective control and jurisdiction over that part of Korea where the United Nations Temporary Commission on Korea was able to observe and consult and in which the great majority of the people of Korea reside; and that this Government is based on elections which were a valid expression of the free will of the electorate of that part of Korea and which were observed by the Temporary Commission; and that this is the only such Government in Korea";

Mindful of the concern expressed by the General Assembly in its resolutions of 12 December 1948 and 21 October 1949 of the consequences which might follow unless Member States refrained from acts derogatory to the results sought to be achieved by the United Nations in bringing about the complete independence and unity of Korea; and the concern expressed that the situation described by the United Nations Commission on Korea in its report menaces the safety and well being of the Republic of Korea and of the people of Korea and might lead to open military conflict there;

Noting with grave concern the armed attack upon the Republic of Korea by forces from North Korea,

Determines that this action constitutes a breach of the peace,

I. Calls for the immediate cessation of hostilities; and
   Calls upon the authorities of North Korea to withdraw forthwith their armed forces to the thirty-eighth parallel;

/II. Requests
S/1501

> S/1501
> Page 2
>
> II. Requests the United Nations Commission on Korea
> (a) To communicate its fully considered recommendations on the situation with the least possible delay;
> (b) To observe the withdrawal of the North Korean forces to the thirty-eighth parallel; and
> (c) To keep the Security Council informed on the execution of this resolution;
>
> III. Calls upon all Members to render every assistance to the United Nations in the execution of this resolution and to refrain from giving assistance to the North Korean authorities.

참고 1. S-1501 RESOLUTION CONCERNING THE COMPLAINT OF AGGRESSION UPON THE REPUBLIC OF KOREA ADOPTED AT THE 473RD MEETING OF THE SECURITY COUNCIL ON 25 JUNE 1950

게다가 트루먼 행정부는 남한의 이승만 정권에 미군 무기를 보내고 미 공군과 해군에 인민군을 공격하도록 명령함으로써 안보리결의 82호를 즉시 남용했습니다. 1950년 6월 27일 트루먼 대통령은 다음과 같이 말했습니다.

> "안전보장이사회는 유엔의 모든 회원국들에게 이 결의(6월25일)의 실행에 있어 유엔에 모든 지원을 제공할 것을 요청했다. 이런 상황에서 나는 미 공군과 해군에게 한국 정부군을 엄호하고 지원하도록 명령했다."

이 성명은 트루먼 행정부가 안보리결의 82호의 3조에 있는 "모든 지원"을, 마치 한국방위에 무력 사용을 승인한 것처럼 폭넓게 마구 끌어대는 방식으로 해석했음을 보여줍니다. 이는 양측에 "적대행위의 즉각적인 중단"과 "38선까지" 북한군의 철수를 호소했을 뿐인 결의 82호의 노골적인 왜곡 외에 아무것도 아닙니다.

---

5   S/1501

6   SCR은 Security Council Resolution(안보리결의)의 약자이다. 즉 안보리결의 번호로는 82호가 되고 안보리 공식문서 일련번호로는 S/1501이 됨을 의미하는 것으로 번호만 다를 뿐 같은 내용이다.

"적대행위 중단" 요청은 한국의 두 정부를 포함할 뿐 아니라 미국 정부를 포함한 그들의 군사동맹 모두에 적용됩니다. 한국에서의 무력사용에 대한 안보리결의 이전인 6월 27일~28일(한국 시간) 북한군을 공격함으로써 트루먼 행정부는 조선민주주의인민공화국에 대한 침략과 안보리결의 82호의 위반을 승인하였습니다.

트루먼 행정부의 북한에 대한 신속하고 일방적인 군사행동은 당시 그 영향력을 과소평가할 수 없습니다. 이러한 움직임은 한국 내전으로 간주되던 것을 극동의 강대국이 참여하는 위험한 국제전으로 전환시켰습니다. 위험한 조치를 취하면서 미국 정부는 유엔헌장 2조 2,3,4,5,7항을 포함하여 유엔헌장을 광범위하고 심각하게 위반했습니다.

특히 유엔헌장이 유엔의 개별국가에 대한 내정 간섭을 구체적으로 금지하고 있기 때문에 우선 안보리가 한국 분쟁에 간섭할 수 있는 관할권이 있는지 여부에 대한 의구심이 많습니다. 유엔헌장 제2조7항은 다음과 같이 명시하고 있습니다.

> "본 헌장에 포함된 어떠한 것도 유엔이 본질적으로 어느 국가의 국내관할권에 속한 문제에 개입할 수 있는 권한을 부여하지 않는다. 그러나 이 원칙은 제7장의 강제조치가 실행되는 것을 방해하지 않는다."

1948년 한국에 두개의 국가가 등장했을 때, 남한의 대한민국(ROK)이나 북한의 조선민주주의인민공화국(DPRK)은 상대 정부를 인정하지 않았습니다. 각각은 한국 전체를 대표한다고 주장했습니다. 천 년이 넘는 통일한국의 오랜 역사를 생각하면 이것은 놀라운 일이 아닙니다. 트루먼 행정부 자체가 대한민국을 (주권은 남한에 국한되지만) 한국의 유일한 합법정부로 간주했던 반면 조선민주주의인민공화국은 법적 독립국가로 인정하지 않았습니다. 이에 트루먼 대통령은 6월 29일 기자회견에서 한국 상황을 다음과 같이 설명했습니다.

> "(대한민국)은 이웃인 반도들에게 불법적으로 공격당했다…그리고 유엔회원국들도 대한민국에 대한 반도들의 습격을 진압하기 위해 대한민국을 구호할 것이다."

달리 말하면, 트루먼과 그의 참모들은 6월에 발생한 한국의 무력충돌이 단지 국내적 혼란에 불과하다는 입장을 취했습니다.

이와 유사한 입장을 취하고 있는 미 국무부의 안보리결의 82호 초안 역시 트루먼의 견해를 반영하고 있습니다. 즉, 한국 분쟁은 "북한군대"라 부르는 조선민주주의인민공화국의 조선인민군과 "북한당국"이라 부르는 조선민주주의인민공화국에 의한 내부 반란이라는 것입니다. 한편, 안보리는 결의 82호를 채택하면서 한국에 '평화의 파괴'가 존재한다고 결정함으로써 한국 분쟁의 본질에 대해 다른 입장을 취했습니다. 유엔법 전문가인 한스 켈젠 교수에 따르면 '평화의 파괴'에 대한 안보리의 초기 결정은 실수였습니다.

> "평화 또는 헌장이 말하는 '국제평화'는 국가 간의 관계이다. 따라서 '평화의 파괴'는 한 국가의 다른 국가와의 관계에서만 인정될 수 있다. '북한군대'가 한 국가의 군대가 아니라면, 그리고 '북한당국'이 한 국가의 정부가 아니라 혁명집단이나 반란군이라면, 그리하여 결과적으로 한국전쟁이 내전이라면, 안보리는 평화의 파괴의 존재를 결정할 수 없다. 그것은 단지 평화에 대한 위협을 결정할 수 있을 뿐이다."[7]

당시 한국 상황에서 국제평화의 파괴나 국제평화의 위협의 존재를 결정할 타당한 근거가 없었기 때문에 유엔은 1950년 6월 한국의 국내 분쟁에 개입할 법적 권한이 전혀 없었습니다. 당시 한국 상황에서는 유엔헌장 2조 7항에 따른 "제7장에 따른 강제조치"를 제외하고는 어떤 개입도 적법

---

[7] Hans Kelsen, *Law of the United Nations*, (New York: Frederick A. Praeger, 1951), p.930

하지 않았습니다. 그럼에도 불구하고 트루먼 행정부는 한국 문제를 유엔에 제출했는데, 이는 미국 관리들이 안보리에서 그들이 원하는 결의안을 통과시키기 위해 필요한 표를 가지고 있다고 - 특히 당시 소련이 안보리 회의를 보이콧하고 있던 사실로부터 - 확신했기 때문입니다. 또한 미국 정부가 한국, 일본, 미국 및 기타 국가의 국민들에 대한 선전을 목적으로 유엔 경찰조치로서 한국전쟁을 묘사하는 것도 매우 유용했습니다.

2. 1950년 6월 27일 안보리결의 83호의 문제점

6월 27일, 안보리는 유엔한국위원단이 "양 당사자가 평화협상을 위한 중립적 중재자에 동의하거나 회원국 정부들에 즉각적인 중재를 수행하기 위해"[8] 양측의 초청을 고려하도록 안보리에 제안하는 몇 개의 전신을 검토하기 위해 한국 상황에 대한 두 번째 회의를 개최하였습니다. 미국 대표는 이 제안을 무시하고 유엔회원국들에게 "이 지역의 국제평화와 안보를 회복하고 무력공격을 격퇴하는데 필요한 지원을 대한민국에 제공"할 것을 권고한 또 다른 결의안을 서둘러 제출했습니다.

무력의 사용에 의한 직접적인 유엔 강제조치를 명시적으로 허용하는 유일한 조항은 헌장 제7장 42조이지만 트루먼 행정부는 군사조치에 있어 최대한의 자유 유지, 유엔군 창설 시간 부족 등 여러 가지 이유로 한국 분쟁을 처리하는 데 헌장 제42조의 인용을 꺼렸습니다.

따라서 미국 정부는 결국 유엔 역사상 처음으로 제39조의 "권고" 문구를 사용하게 되었습니다. 그러나 켈젠 교수는 유엔헌장의 초안자들이 그러한 "권고"가 무력의 사용을 포함하는 것으로 의도하지 않았다고 합니다.

---

8 S/1503, June 26, 1950

따라서 그는 안보리가 국제평화의 위협이나 파괴가 존재한다고 결정하면, "제39조에 따라" 안보리는 "강제조치를 권고할 수 없으며, 상황 조절을 위한 평화적 수단만 권고할 수 있다"고 말합니다.[9] 따라서 유엔회원국들에게 암묵적으로 무력 사용을 권고한 안보리결의 83호는, 유엔헌장 작성자들의 원래 의도에 따라 엄격하게 해석한다면, 불법입니다.

결의 83호의 두 번째 문제는 본질적 문제에 대한 안보리의 결정이 헌장 제27조 3항에 따라 '상임이사의 동의를 포함하여' 당시 7명 위원의 찬성을 필요로 한다는 점입니다. 그래서 소련은 결의 83호가 "안보리 상임이사국인 소련과 중국"(중화인민공화국)의 결석 상태에서 채택되었기 때문에 불법이라고 6월 29일 유엔에 통보했습니다. 소련은 또한 안보리결의 83호가 장개석 대표의 표를 포함하지 않는다면 단 6표의 찬성으로 채택되었기 때문에 불법이라고 문제제기했습니다.[10]

소련은 1950년 1월 중순부터 대만 장개석정권 대표가 안보리 의석을 계속 유지하는 것에 항의하여 안보리 회의에 불참하고 있었습니다.

불행히도 안보리의 어떤 회원국도 안보리결의 83호 초안이 검토될 당시 이러한 법적 문제에 대해 질문을 제기하지 않았습니다. 게다가 미 공군과 해군에 북한군에 대한 폭격을 명령했다는 트루먼의 6월 27일 정오(미국 동부시각)에 나온 공식 발표를 감히 비판하는 회원국은 없었습니다. 이 명령은 안보리결의 83호가 채택되기 훨씬 전에, 헌장 2조4항을 포함, 많은 조항을 위반하여 하달되었습니다. 그 결과 6월 27일 오후 안보리회의는 미국정부에 의한 한국에서의 일방적 무력 사용을 승인하는 형식적 날인 절차로 변질되었습니다.

---

[9] Kelsen, p.932
[10] S/1517

강력한 미국의 압력 아래 안보리결의 83호는 결국 같은 날 오후 11시경 유고슬라비아의 반대 1표, 기권 2표(이집트와 인도)로 채택되었습니다. (참고.2, SCR 83, S/1511, June 27, 1950)

참고 2. S-1511 SECURITY COUNCIL RESOLUTION 83 (1950) [ON ASSISTANCE TO THE REPUBLIC OF KOREA], 1950.6.27

트루먼 행정부는 이 결의안을 빨리 통과시키려고, 이집트와 인도 정부가 결의안을 검토하고 뉴욕에 있는 대표자들에게 지시를 보낼 충분한 시간조차 허용하지 않았습니다. 또한 대한민국 대표가 안보리회의에 앉아 군사원조를 강력히 호소하는 것을 다시 허용했지만, 회의에서 발언하도록 조선민주주의인민공화국 대표를 초청하지는 않았습니다.

한국 분쟁이 심화되어가는 이 위급한 시간에 트루먼의 오만과 위선은 절정에 다다랐습니다. 그는 6월 27일 공식발표에서 "미국은 법에 의한 지배를 계속 옹호할 것이다"라고 천명하면서, 한편에서는 유엔헌장과 미국헌법을 갈기갈기 찢어버렸습니다.[11]

3. 1950년 7월 7일 안보리결의 84호의 문제점

당시 초대 유엔사무총장은 자서전에서, 한국에서의 유엔 노력을 위한 "일부 조정 메커니즘"을 만들기 위해 새로운 안보리 결의안을 준비한 것은 그와 그의 고문들이며, "7월 3일에 미국, 영국, 프랑스 대표단과 안전보장이사회 의장 노르웨이 아르네 순데에게 회람시켰다"고 주장했습니다.

그의 제안은 7개의 유엔회원국으로 구성된 안보리 "한국지원조정위원회"를 설립하여 회원국의 다양한 군대를 조정하고 감독하는 것이었습니다. 그의 제안은 또한 이 결의에 따라 행동하는 자발적인 유엔회원국의 연합군이 유엔기를 사용하도록 승인하는 것이었습니다.

사무총장 트리그브 리는 영국, 프랑스, 노르웨이가 "이런 위원회의 아이디어를 좋아했다"고 말했습니다. 그러나 "미 국방부가 그러한 유엔 조치에 많

---

[11] "트루먼대통령 공식발표 자료", *UPI*, (1950.6.27.)

은 반대"를 했기 때문에 "미국 대표는 즉시 말을 바꿨다"고 말했습니다.[12]

어쨌든 안보리가 유엔헌장 7장의 중요 위반을 초래할 그런 단계에서 리가 그런 대담한 제안을 한 것은 꽤 놀랍습니다. 7월 3일 애치슨 미 국무장관도 유엔주재 미국 대표에게 후반의 의견과 관련하여, 한국에 대한 새로운 결의안을 보냈다는 점이 흥미롭습니다. 이 초안은 유엔깃발 사용에 관한 내용이 없고 리가 제안한 안보리의 위원회가 실질적 권한이 없다는 점을 명시한 걸 빼고는 최종 안보리결의 84호의 주요 내용을 유지했습니다.[13]

미국 대표가 리와 미국 초안을 공유했는지 여부는 명확하지 않습니다. 미국정부와의 긴밀한 관계를 고려할 때 트리그브 리는 미국 초안을 보고 자신의 초안으로 수정했을 가능성이 꽤 큽니다. 사무총장은 단지 유엔의 "행정관리"일 뿐이므로 사무총장이 안보리 결의안을 배포하는 것은 매우 드문 일이었습니다.

어쨌든 미 국무부는 7월 4일 유엔기 사용 등 트리그브 리의 일부 제안을 반영해 결의안을 수정했습니다. 7월 6일, 유엔안보리 의장은 결의안(3) 문단 끝에 "유엔을 위한 기구로서"라는 문구를 추가해줄 수 있는지 유엔 미국 대표에 문의했습니다. 그러나 이 제안은 미국 대표에 의해 거부되었습니다.[14]

결국 최종 결의안은 안보리 내에 조정위원회를 설치하는 어떤 언급도 삭제했습니다. 따라서 안보리는 7월 7일 미국을 위해 최대한의 자유를 제공한 결의84호를 채택했습니다. (참고.3, S/1588 1950.7.7)

---

[12] Trygve Lie, *In the Cause of Peace*, (New York: Macmillan Co, 1954), pp.333-334
[13] *Foreign Relations United States* (*FRUS*), 1950, Korea, Vol. VII, Doc. 206
[14] *FRUS*, 1950, Korea, Vol. VII, Doc. 229

```
UNITED NATIONS                                      GENERAL
SECURITY                                            S/1588
                                                    7 July 1950
COUNCIL                                             ORIGINAL: ENGLISH-
                                                              FRENCH
```

RESOLUTION CONCERNING THE COMPLAINT OF AGGRESSION UPON THE
REPUBLIC OF KOREA ADOPTED AT THE 476TH MEETING OF THE
SECURITY COUNCIL ON 7 JULY 1950

The Security Council,

Having determined that the armed attack upon the Republic of Korea by forces from North Korea constitutes a breach of the peace,

Having recommended that Members of the United Nations furnish such assistance to the Republic of Korea as may be necessary to repel the armed attack and to restore international peace and security in the area,

1. Welcomes the prompt and vigorous support which governments and peoples of the United Nations have given to its Resolutions of 25 and 27 June 1950 to assist the Republic of Korea in defending itself against armed attack and thus to restore international peace and security in the area;

2. Notes that Members of the United Nations have transmitted to the United Nations offers of assistance for the Republic of Korea;

3. Recommends that all Members providing military forces and other assistance pursuant to the aforesaid Security Council resolutions make such forces and other assistance available to a unified command under the United States;

4. Requests the United States to designate the commander of such forces;

5. Authorizes the unified command at its discretion to use the United Nations flag in the course of operations against North Korean forces concurrently with the flags of the various nations participating;

6. Requests the United States to provide the Security Council with reports as appropriate on the course of action taken under the unified command.

참고 3. S-1588 RESOLUTION CONCERNING THE COMPLAINT OF AGGRESSION UPON THE REPUBLIC OF KOREA ADOPTED AT THE 478TH MEETING OF THE SECURITY COUNCIL ON 7 JULY 1950

외양을 위해 트루먼 행정부는 영국과 프랑스의 유엔 주재 대표들에게 새로운 안보리 결의안을 공동 지원할 것을 요청했고 그들은 그렇게 하기로 동의했습니다. 그러나 소련은 아직 안보리 회의에 참석하지 않았고 존경받는 세 유엔회원국(이집트, 인도, 유고슬라비아)은 투표에서 기권했으며 결의안에 대한 명백한 반대를 보여주었습니다. 그들의 우려는 무엇이었을까요?

그들은 유엔기의 사용을 포함, 유엔헌장에 따른 이 결의안의 적법성에 대해 심각한 의문을 품었을 것입니다. 그들의 기권투표는 트루먼 행정부가 이 결의안을 마음대로 남용하기 시작한 것이 곧 밝혀졌기 때문에 완전히 정당화되었습니다.

결의 84호3항은 안보리가 "군대를 제공하는 모든 회원국이… 그런 병력을… 미국의 통합사령부가 이용하도록 할 것을 권고한다"고 명시하고 있으며, 4항은 안보리에 "미국에 그런 군대의 사령관을 지명할 것을 요청한다"고 명시했습니다.

이 결의안을 해석함에 있어 이 문서가 모든 회원국을 구속하는 것은 아니라는 점에 유의하는 것이 중요합니다. 한국에 군대나 기타 지원을 보낼지 여부를 결정하는 것은 각 회원국의 몫이었습니다. 또한, 안보리결의 84호는 유엔 회원국이 남한에 파견하는 군대와 관련하여 "유엔군"이라는 표현을 사용하지 않았다는 점도 유의해야 합니다. 더욱이 이 결의안에는 "유엔사령관"의 직함이나 "유엔사령부"의 명칭에 대해서는 언급된 바가 없습니다. 그렇다면 이런 직함과 이름은 누가 만든 것일까요?

1950년 7월 8일 트루먼 대통령은 자신이 더글러스 맥아더 장군을 "미국의 통합사령부 하에 배치하는 유엔회원국 군대의 총사령관"으로 지명했다고 발표했습니다. 이어 7월 10일 미국합동참모본부(JCS)는 극동사령부에 공식 메시지를 보내 맥아더가 대통령에 의해 "미국통합사령부 하에 배치된 대한민국을 지원하는 군대의 사령관"으로 지명됐다"고 전했습니다. (참고.4, JCS 메시지, 1950년 7월 10일, Truman Library)

여기서도 합참 메시지에는 "유엔사"에 대한 언급이 없습니다. 그러나 답장으로 맥아더는 7월 11일 트루먼에게 "한국에서 근무하게 된 국제군대

DEPARTMENT OF THE ARMY
STAFF MESSAGE CENTER
OUTGOING CLASSIFIED MESSAGE

~~SECRET~~
OPERATIONAL IMMEDIATE

PARAPHRASE NOT REQUIRED

Joint Chiefs of Staff
M M Stephens Capt US Navy
Executive Secretary JCS
55234

TO: CINCFE TOKYO JAPAN

INFO: CINCAL FT RICHARDSON ALASKA, CINCARIB QUARRY HEIGHTS CZ, CINCEUR HEIDELBERG GERMANY, COMGENUSFA (REAR) SALZBURG AUSTRIA, CINCPAC PEARL HARBOR TH, CINCIANT NORFOLK VA, CINCNELM LONDON ENGLAND, COMGENSAC OFFUTT AFB OMAHA NEBR, COMGENTRUST TRIESTE.

NR: JCS 85370   10 JUL 50

From JCS.

    You have been designated by the President of the United States as commander of military forces assisting the Republic of Korea which are placed under the unified command of the United States by members of the United Nations in response to the resolution of 7 July of the Security Council of the United Nations. You are authorized to use at your discretion the United Nations flag concurrently with the flags of other nations participating in operations against North Korean forces. The United Nations flag will be used only in operations against North Korean forces and will therefore not be used in connection with your mission with respect to Formosa.

    The terms of this directive authorizing the use of the United Nations flag at your discretion have been approved by the President of the United States and supersede the implications in his press release, Washington, 8 July, (Info note: Text of Security Council resolution of 7 July will be transmitted to you).

ORIGIN: JCS

DISTR: NAVAIDE, CSAF, CNO, CSA

CM OUT 85370   (Jul 50)   DTG: 101714Z   rkh

DECLASSIFIED
E.O. 12065, Sec. 3-402
DOD Directive 5100.30, June 18, 1979
By NLT- _____ NARS, Date 11-5-__

COPY NO. M-2

THE MAKING OF AN EXACT COPY OF THIS MESSAGE IS FORBIDDEN

참고 4. JCS 메시지, 1950년 7월 10일, Truman Library

의 유엔사령관"으로 그를 임명한 트루먼에게 감사하는 개인적 편지를 전했습니다. (참고.5, MacArthur's Message, 1950년 7월 11일, Truman Library)

같은 날 트루먼은 맥아더에게 "주한 국제군대의 유엔사령관"으로서 장군의 임명과 관련한 맥아더의 메시지에 감사를 표하는 개인 메시지를 보냈

```
                        SIGNAL CENTER
                          EAST WING
                        The White House

                                        11 July 1950

        TO   : THE PRESIDENT
        FROM : General Douglas MacArthur

             PERSONAL FOR PRESIDENT HARRY S TRUMAN

             Dear Mr President:
                         I have just received the announcement of your
        appointment of me as the United Nations Commander of the international
        forces to be employed in Korea and can not fail to express to you
        personally my deepest thanks and appreciation for this new expression
        of your confidence. I recall so vividly and with such gratitude that
        this is the second time you have so signally honored me. Your personal
        choice five years ago as Supreme Commander for the Allied Powers in Japan
        placed me under an intimate obligation which would be difficult for me
        to ever repay and you have now added to my debt. I can only repeat the
        pledge of my complete personal loyalty to you as well as an absolute
        devotion to your monumental struggle for peace and good will throughout
        the world. I hope I will not fail you.

                                Most respectfully and faithfully,
                                   (Signed)  Douglas MacArthur

        Recd 110255Z/too late for delivery/ Capt. Dudley
```

참고 5. MacArthur's Message, 1950년 7월 11일, Truman Library

습니다. (참고.6, Truman's Message, 1950년 7월 11일, Truman Library)

따라서 자신의 직함을 "유엔사령관"으로 사용하기 시작한 것은 맥아더 자신이었고 트루먼은 맥아더에게 보낸 그의 개인 메시지에서 그 직함을 단지 확인했습니다.

MESSAGES BETWEEN THE PRESIDENT AND GENERAL MACARTHUR

SIGNAL CENTER
EAST WING
The White House

11 July, 1950

TO : General Douglas MacArthur
FROM : The President
NR : WH 497   Filed 112035Z

Dear General MacArthur:

I deeply appreciate the letter and the spirit of your message relating to your appointment as the United Nations Commander of the international forces in Korea. Your words confirm me dash if any confirmation were needed dash in my full belief in the wisdom of your selection.

With my warm regards and all good wishes,
I am

Sincerely yours,

Harry S. Truman

참고 6. Truman's Message, 1950년 7월 11일, Truman Library

그러나 달리 말하는 트루먼의 막역한 친구 한 명이 있습니다. 1950년 상원 외교관계위원회 위원장 톰 코넬리 상원의원에 따르면 트루먼은 1950년 6월 30일 한국 문제에 대한 백악관 브리핑에서 그와 의회의 다른 중요 인사들에게 "맥아더는 미국사령관으로서 뿐만 아니라 유엔사령관으로서도 싸우고 있다"고 말했습니다.[15]

만약 이것이 사실이라면 이후의 모든 것에서 트루먼 자신이 최초로 유엔 직함을 사용하기 시작한 것입니다.

"유엔사령부"란 명칭 자체는 1950년 7월 25일 더글러스 맥아더 장군의 이름으로 도쿄에서 별도의 군사령부로 공식적으로 사용되기 시작했습니다. (참고.7, S/1629, 한국 시간으로 1950년 7월 25일)

그러나 "유엔사"에는 별도의 참모나 시설이 없었습니다. "유엔사"의 거의 모든 참모들은 당시 도쿄에 있는 미 극동사령부 참모장교로 근무하고 있던 미군 장교들 중에서 선발됐습니다.

"유엔사" 이름을 사용하는 것은 유엔 이름을 고의적으로 남용하는 것에 지나지 않습니다. 맥아더가 자신의 주도로 이름을 사용했는지 아니면 워싱턴의 명령에 따라 이름을 사용했는지는 분명하지 않습니다. 앞서 언급했듯이 7월 10일 합참 메시지나 7월 8일 트루먼의 발표는 맥아더에게 특별히 도쿄에 "유엔사"를 설립하도록 지시하지 않았습니다. 그러나 맥아더가 트루먼의 명령에 따라 행동했음을 확인하는 미군 역사책 한 권이 있습니다.

> "7월 10일 유엔의 요청에 따라 트루먼 대통령은 맥아더 장군에게 유엔사령부(UNC)를 설립하도록 지시했다…"[16]

---

[15] Tom Connally, *My Name is Tom Connally*, (Thomas Y. Crowell Company, 1954), p.349

[16] Joint History Office, Office of the Chairman of the Joint Chiefs of Staff, *The History of the Unified Command Plan*, 1946-1999, (2003), p.19

```
UNITED NATIONS
SECURITY                            GENERAL
COUNCIL                                                 S/1629
                                                        25 July 1950
                                                        ORIGINAL: ENGLISH
```

NOTE DATED 25 JULY 1950 FROM THE REPRESENTATIVE OF THE UNITED STATES OF
AMERICA TO THE SECRETARY-GENERAL TRANSMITTING THE TEXT
OF COMMUNIQUE NUMBER 135 OF THE FAR EAST COMMAND

The Representative of the United States to the United Nations presents his compliments to the Secretary-General of the United Nations and has the honour to request that there be brought to the attention of the Security Council the following Far East Command Communiqué Number 135:

(Released Tokyo 0850 Korean Time 25 July (EDT 1850 24 July))

The United Nations Command, with General Headquarters in Tokyo, was officially established today with General Douglas MacArthur as Commander-in-Chief The announcement was made in General Order No. 1, General Headquarters, United Nations Command. The order reads:

"1. In response to the resolution of the Security Council of the United Nations of July 7, 1950, the President of the United States has designated the undersigned Commander-in-Chief of the Military Forces assisting the Republic of Korea. Pursuant thereto, there is established this date the United Nations Command, with General Headquarters in Tokyo, Japan.

"2. The undersigned assumes command.

"Douglas MacArthur
General of the Army,
United States Army
Commander-in-Chief"

참고 7. S_1629-UNC창설보고1950.7.25

이 책의 서술은 문제의 트루먼 명령이 포함된 기밀문서를 기반으로 했을 가능성이 있지만 그런 문서는 아직 일반에 공개되지 않았습니다. 이와 관련하여 트루먼 자신이 "통합사령부"와 "유엔사령부"의 관계를 어떻게 보았는지 주목하는 것은 흥미롭습니다. 회고록에서 그는 다음과 같이 말했습니다.

"우리는 한국에서 유엔을 대신하여 유엔의 이름으로 존재했다. 내가 더글라스 맥아더에게 위임한 '통합사령부'는 유엔사령부였다."[17]

즉, 그는 두 이름이 동전의 앞뒷면과 같다고 말하고 있는 것이며 그는 적어도 "유엔사령부"라는 명칭을 승인했습니다.

그럼에도 불구하고 이 이야기에는 또 다른 반전이 있습니다. 유엔본부 미국 상임대표 오스틴 대사는 1950년 7월 31일 안보리 회의에서 "유엔사"는 단지 미국통합사령부 산하의 "야전기관"일 뿐이라고 설명했습니다. 그것은 충격적인 진술이었지만 미국 고위관리에 의해 "유엔사"라는 이름을 그들의 목적에 따라 도용했다는 간접적 인정이었습니다.

이러한 명칭은 한국에 대한 미군의 개입을 유엔 임무로서 그리고 "유엔군"으로서 묘사하기 위한 의도임이 분명했습니다. 사실 미국통합사령부가 안보리에 제출한 첫 번째 보고서에서는 한국에서 싸우는 다국적 군대를 "통합사령부 군대" 뿐만 아니라 "유엔군"으로 묘사했습니다.[18]

아마도 "유엔사" 이름을 사용한 또 다른 이유는 다른 회원국들이 유엔의 이름으로 한국에 군대를 파병하는 것을 더 쉽게 하려 함이었을 것입니다. 또한 한국군이 미국 작전통제 하에 들어가는 것을 더 쉽게 하려 함이었을 것입니다.

결의 84호5항은 안보리가 "북한군에 대한 작전 과정에서 유엔기 사용에 대해 통합사령부의 재량에 따를 것을 승인한다"라고 명시하고 있습니다. 확실히 이 단락은 결의 84호에서 가장 문제가 되는 부분일 것입니다. 여기서 주된 문제는 안보리가 1950년에 한국에서 군사작전에 개입하게 될

---

17 Harry S. Truman, *Memoirs by Harry S. Truman*, Vol.2, (William S. Konecky Associates, 1956), p.378
18 S/1626, 1950년 7월 25일, 미국동부표준시

다국적군 통합사령부에 유엔기 사용을 승인할 권한이 있었는지 여부입니다. 대답은 두 가지 주요 이유에서 "아니오"입니다.

첫째, 유엔헌장 5장 또는 7장에 따라 안보리가 유엔깃발의 사용을 통제할 수 있는 특별한 권한은 없습니다. 실제로 안보리는 안보리결의 84호의 5항을 채택함으로써 유엔기와 유엔기법을 채택하도록 사무총장에게 권한을 부여한 1947년 10월 총회결의 167(II)을 위반했습니다. 총회결의에 따라 트리그브 리 사무총장은 1947년 12월에 최초의 유엔기법을 발표했습니다. 그러나 이 법에는 군사작전에서의 유엔기 사용에 대한 조항이 포함되어 있지 않았습니다. 결의 84호가 채택된 지 약 20일이 지난 1950년 7월 28일, 사무총장은 유엔기법에 깃발은 "유엔의 관할기관에 의해 그 효력에 대한 명시적인 승인이 있어야만 군사작전에 사용될 수 있다"(유엔기법6항)는 새로운 단락을 추가하였습니다.

그럼에도 불구하고 켈젠 교수는 새 단락을 결 84호5항의 '사후적' 정당화라고 비판했으며, 7월 7일 당시 "기의 사용을 승인할 권한이 있는 유엔기관은 유엔사무총장뿐"이라고 상기시켰습니다.[19]

따라서 리 사무총장이 다른 유엔기관에 그의 권한을 위임하려는 시도는 총회결의 167(II)을 위반했기 때문에 무효, 무익한 것이었습니다. 비유엔기구인 통합사령부에 유엔깃발 사용을 승인하려는 트리그브 리의 노력과 7월 7일 안보리의 조치를 정당화하기 위해 유엔깃발법을 수정한 그의 조치는 유엔의 이익과 존엄을 훼손했을 뿐이므로 상당히 비난받을 만합니다.

둘째, 유엔기의 계속 사용과 관련하여 북한군에 대한 군사작전이 없는 이 시점에서 한국의 "유엔사"와 일본의 "유엔사 후방기지"가 여전히 유엔기를

---

[19] Kelsen, p.938

사용할 수 있는지에 대한 또 다른 법적 문제가 있습니다. 5항의 언어는 통합사령부가 "북한군에 대한 작전 중에"만 유엔기를 사용할 수 있다고 명시하고 있습니다. 이 단락은 영국과 프랑스 대표가 유엔기 사용을 제한하려는 노력의 일환으로 5번 항목에 추가했기 때문에 좁게 해석해야 합니다.[20] 이는 "유엔사"와 "유엔사 후방기지"가 1953년 정전협정으로 한국에서의 전투가 중단되었을 때 유엔깃발 사용을 중단했어야 함을 의미합니다.

이에 따라 2019년 9월 한국 및 기타 세계 46개 시민사회단체가 국제민주법률가협회(IADL)와 함께 구테레스 유엔사무총장에게 보내는 서한에서

오키나와 캠프화이트비치에 게양되어 있는 유엔기

20 *FRUS*, Doc. 229 참조

ASSOCIATION INTERNATIONALE DES JURISTES DEMOCRATES • ASOCIACIÓN INTERNACIONAL DE JURISTAS DEMOCRATAS • МЕЖДУНАРОДНОЙ АССОЦИАЦИИ ЮРИСТОВ-ДЕМОКРАТОВ • 国际民主法律家协会

CHAUSÉE DE HAECHT 55, 1210, BRUXELLES-BRUSSELS. BELGIQUE-BELGIUM
info@iadllaw.org www.iadllaw.org

September 30, 2019

Hon. Antonio Guterres
Secretary-General
The United Nations
New York, New York
Sgcentral@un.org

Re: Seeking the Position of the UN Secretary-General on the Use of the UN Flag by the "United Nations Command" in Korea and Japan

Dear Secretary-General Guterres:

The International Association of Democratic Lawyers, (IADL) a non-governmental organization with consultative status with ECOSOC, is writing on behalf of itself and other civil society groups that are supporting this letter (the list of these groups is at p. 3). We are seeking your opinion on the above issue because the UN General Assembly adopted a resolution beginning in its early history to protect the name of the United Nations and Secretary-General had been authorized by the General Assembly to adopt a UN flag code and protect its dignity.[1]

1. The U.S. military is still using the UN flag at certain military bases in Korea and Japan, in claiming to be the "United Nations Command," which was unilaterally created by the U.S. in July 1950. The U.S. uses Security Council Resolution 84 of 7 July 1950 to justify its use of the UN flag. However, there are some serious problems with such use. For instance, the Security Council made a grave mistake in authorizing the use of the UN flag for a non-UN, multi-national military command that was only recommended in SCR 84. Perhaps, some members of the Security Council at the time may have believed that the Security Council had such power. However, according to Prof. Hans Kelsen, the leading legal scholar on the Charter and Law of the United Nations at the time, such opinion had "no basis neither in the Charter nor in the Resolution 167(II) of the General Assembly."[2] Moreover, SCR 84 authorized the "Unified Command" to use the UN flag in the "course of operations against North Korean forces," but the U.S. military has used the UN flag in the name of the "UN Command" in its military operations in Korea from the beginning.

2. The first UN Flag Code was issued on 19 December 1947, and Pt. 8 of the Code stated that "the flag shall not be used except in accordance with this Flag Code." However, the Code did not contain a provision authorizing the use of the flag in military operations. On 28 July, 1950, Secretary-General Trygve Lie added to the Code a new paragraph under Pt. 6 which stipulated that "the flag may be used in military operations only upon express authorization to that effect by a

[1] A/RES/92 (I), Official Seal and Emblem of the UN, 7 December, 1946; A/RES/167 (II), United Nations Flag, 20 October 1947.
[2] Hans Kelsen, *The Law of the United Nations: A Critical Analysis of Its Fundamental Problems* (New York: Frederick A. Praeger, 1950), p. 938.

1

참고 8. 2019년 9월 30일 UN사무총장에게 보내는 IADL 서신

한국과 일본의 "유엔사"에 의해 유엔깃발의 사용이 지속되는 데 대한 의견을 물었습니다. (참고.8, 2019년 9월 30일 UN사무총장에게 보내는 IADL 서신)

그러나 유엔법무차관보는 2019년 10월 "문의하신 질문이 사무총장의 권

참고 9. Response from Mr. Mathias-UNC

한에 속하지 않는 문제"라는 짧은 편지로 답변했습니다. (참고.9, UN사무국 답신, 2019년 10월 10일)

불행히도 회피성 편지는 그 결론의 법적 근거를 설명하지 못했고 유엔깃발 사용을 승인하는 권한이 1946년 12월 7일 유엔총회결의 92(I), 1947년 10월 20일 167(II)에 의해 사무총장에게 위임되어 있다는 사실을 무시하였습니다. 그러나 유엔사무총장은 2019년 서한에서 제기된 우리의 지적을 일부 받아들인 듯, 2020년 11월 20일 1967년 이후 53년 만에 유엔기법을 개정했습니다. 이에 따라 "유엔사"는 한국과 일본에서 유엔기를 계속 사용하는 것에 대해 유엔으로부터 강력한 도전에 직면하게 되었습니다. 우리는 개정된 유엔기법을 우리 운동의 첫 번째 성과로 생각하며 적극 환영합니다. (참고.10, ST/SGB/2020/4 개정된 유엔기법 2020.11.20.)

United Nations  Secretariat

ST/SGB/2020/4

20 November 2020

Secretary-General's bulletin

United Nations Flag Code

The Secretary-General, for the purpose of updating the provisions related to the protocol and use of the flag of the United Nations, hereby promulgates the following:

1. By resolution 167 (II), the General Assembly resolved that the flag of the United Nations shall be the official emblem as adopted in its resolution 92 (I), centred on a light blue background. By the same resolution, the General Assembly directed the Secretary-General to draw up regulations concerning the dimensions and proportions of the flag and authorized the Secretary-General to adopt a flag code, having in mind the desirability of the regulated use of the flag and the protection of its dignity.

2. Pursuant to that resolution, the Flag Code was first issued by the Secretary-General on 19 December 1947 and the Flag Consolidated Regulations on 23 July 1949.

3. The Code and Regulations were amended on 11 November 1952. The Regulations were further revised on 1 January 1967 and the Code and Regulations were promulgated as Secretary-General's bulletin ST/SGB/132.

4. The revised Flag Code, which consolidates the previously separate Flag Code and Flag Regulations into a single document, regulates the use of the flag and is annexed to the present bulletin.

5. The present bulletin shall take effect on the date of its issuance.

6. The Secretary-General's bulletin of 1 January 1967 entitled "The United Nations Flag Code and Regulations" (ST/SGB/132) is hereby abolished.

(*Signed*) António **Guterres**
Secretary-General

참고 10. ST/SGB/2020/4 개정된 유엔기법 2020.11.20.

비무장지대 유엔깃발내리기를 상상하라 - 연천 태풍전망대에 게양되어 있는 유엔깃발

비록 잘 알려지지는 않았지만 유엔 법무국은 실제로 통합사령부와 "유엔사령부"와 유엔의 관계를 검토하고 이 법적 문제를 1994년 법률각서에 명확히 했습니다.

이 법률각서의 핵심 결론은 다음과 같습니다.

1) "안보리가 통합사령부를 그 통제 하에 있는 보조기관으로 설립하지 않았다."
2) "대한민국에 있는 통합사령부는 걸프전에서 세운 동맹 다국적군과 유사하다."
3) "소위 '유엔사령부'는 잘못된 명칭이다."[21]

법률각서 결론의 첫 번째 촛점은 부트로스 부트로스 갈리 당시 유엔사무총장이 1994년 6월 24일 북한 외무상에게 보낸 편지에서 또한 재확인되었습니다. 보다 최근에 유엔과 "유엔사"의 무관성은 유엔 고위관리에 의해 다시 명확해졌습니다.

로즈마리 디칼로 정무사무부총장은 전 유엔본부 미대표부 부대표로 3년 동안 일했습니다. 2018년 안보리 브리핑에서 "유엔사"와 유엔의 관계에 대해 그녀는 다음과 같이 설명했습니다.

"그 이름에도 불구하고, 유엔사령부는 유엔조직이나 기구가 아니며 유엔의 지휘와 통제를 받지도 않는다. 또한 안전보장이사회의 보조기관으로 설립되지 않았으며 유엔 예산을 통해 자금을 지원받지도 않는다. 따라서 유엔사령부와 유엔 사무국사이에는 보고라인이 없다."[22]

---

[21] *UN Juridical Yearbook*, 1994, Chapter VI, pp.501-502
[22] S/PV.8353, 2018년 9월 17일. S는 안보리를, PV는 회의내용을 있는 그대로 기록한 문서형식을 의미합니다.

"유엔사"는 한국주권을 침해했다

1. 미국 통제 하 한국군의 예속

1950년 7월 25일, 미국 대표는 유엔사무총장에게 서한을 제출했는데, 이 서한에서 한국의 이승만 대통령이 1950년 7월 15일 맥아더 장군에게 다음과 같은 편지를 보냈다고 주장했습니다.

> "나는 현재의 적대행위가 계속되는 기간 동안 대한민국의 모든 육, 해, 공군에 대한 일체의 군통수권을 당신에게 이양하게 되어 기쁩니다."

맥아더 또한 7월 18일 무쵸 대사(주한 미대사)에게 메시지를 보내 이승만 대통령에 의해 "취해진 조치에 대한 가장 심오한 존중과 감사"를 전할 것을 요청했습니다.[1] 그러나 역사가들은 이 대통령이 서명한 편지 원본이나 사본을 찾지 못했습니다.

더욱이 두 메시지는 당시 모든 정책사안에 대해 이승만을 긴밀히 응원하거나 지도하고 있던 무쵸 미대사를 통해 교환되어 서한 초안 작성에서 무쵸의 역할 가능성에 대한 의구심을 불러일으켰습니다. 특히 같은 주제에 대해 무쵸가 이승만에게 보낸 편지와 비교할 때 이승만의 편지의 내용과

---

[1] S/1627, 1950년 7월 25일

날짜에 약간의 차이가 있습니다.

예를 들어 무쵸는 '7월 14일'자 이승만의 편지에 답하여, 맥아더가 이승만에게 편지를 보냈다고 한 7월 16일에, 이승만에게 편지를 보냈습니다. 또한, 맥아더의 메시지는 안보리 문서에서 7월 18일자이고, 무쵸의 편지는 7월 16일자입니다.

그의 편지에서 대사는 이승만이 "대한민국의 육, 해, 공군 일체에 대한 작전지휘권을 그(맥아더)에게 지정했다…"고 밝혔습니다. "지정"은 이승만이 유엔에 보낸 편지에서 볼 수 있듯이 "양도"와는 분명히 다릅니다. 유엔에 제출된 문서에는 무쵸가 주장한 것보다 더 광범위한 권한이 포함된 것으로 보입니다. 따라서 이승만 대통령 편지의 실제 내용과 그 메시지가 언제 어떻게 교환되었는지는 명확하지 않습니다.

어쨌든 이승만의 "군통수권" 이양 주장은 한국 헌법상 불법이었는데, 이 중요한 문제는 국무위원들과 결코 논의한 적이 없고, 국무위원들에 의한 어떤 승인 기록이나, 헌법 66조에 의해 요구되는 바 총리나 국방장관에 의한 중요 군사문서에 대한 공동서명도 없었습니다.

더구나 미국과 "유엔사"는 6월 27일 안보리결의안에서 "유엔회원국이 대한민국에 지원을 제공한다…"라고 단지 권고한 특정용어를 위반했습니다. 한국 정부에 필요한 지원을 제공하는 대신 미국 정부와 "유엔사"는 사실, 한국 정부의 모든 통제권-특히 한국군 전체에 대한 통수권-을 1950~1953년의 한국전쟁 3년 동안 장악했습니다.

맥아더 장군으로의 한국군 "통수권" 이양도 또한 심각한 문제를 야기합니다. 이 편지는 이승만이 자진해서 쓴 것일까요, 아니면 미 대사관에서 쓴 것일까요? 이승만 정권의 생존은 미군이 제공하는 도움에 전적으로 의존

했기 때문에 확실히 미국 관리들은 당시 이승만에게 그들의 요구를 명령할 수 있는 위치에 있었습니다. 실제로 주한 미대사, 그의 참모, 맥아더 장군 또는 그의 군대가 이 대통령의 움직임과 결정을 통제하거나 교통부와 통신부를 포함, 다양한 한국 정부기관의 권한을 일방적으로 접수하려고 시도한 사례가 많았습니다. 이승만을 장악함으로써 주한 미대사관은 한국 육군참모총장 채병덕, 내무장관 백성욱을 교체할 정도로 실질적인 지배력을 행사했습니다.

주한 미대사관 제1서기장과 이승만 대통령의 정치연락관으로 재직한 해롤드 J. 노블의 회고록인 「전쟁시 대사관(*Embassy at War*)」의 편집자 프랭크 볼드윈에 따르면, "대사관은 전쟁 노력에 대한 정치적 간섭을 막기 위해 1950년 여름 동안 대통령이 방해가 되지 않기를 원했"습니다.

따라서 존 무쵸 대사는 비록 북한군이 멀리 떨어져 있더라도 이승만이 한 도시에서 다른 도시로 남쪽을 향해 이동할 것을 요구함으로써, 그의 장군들과 국무위원들로부터 격리시키기 위해 노력했습니다. 예를 들어, 이승만은 여름 동안 부산과 대구로 내려가 머무르고 있었습니다. 무쵸가 특히 1950년 6월부터 9월까지 대한민국 대통령 대행을 맡았다고 해도 과언이 아닐 것입니다. 그리고 볼드윈에 따르면 "이승만 대통령은 일시적으로 마지못해 하급 지위를 받아들였다."고 했습니다.[2]

1950년 여름 이승만 대통령과 주한 미 대사관, 주한미군과의 불평등하고 모호한 관계에 대한 위의 이야기는 맥아더 장군에게 한국군 작전통제권을 이양한다는 말과 관련하여 이승만과 맥아더 사이의 의심스런 편지교환이 매우 신뢰할 수 없다는 것을 묘사하고 있습니다.

---

[2] Harold Joyce Noble, Edited by Frank Baldwin, *Embassy at War*, (Seattle: University of Washington Press, 1975), p.xvi

브래들리 장군에 따르면 당시 한국군에게 실제로 일어난 일은 "월튼 워커 (미8군사령관)가 7월 13일 대한민국을 포함한 주한 유엔군 전체의 전술지휘를 맡게 됐다"는 것입니다.³ 따라서 이승만이 맥아더에게 보낸 서명된 편지는 없었을 가능성이 큽니다. 아마도 이승만과 워커 장군, 또는 이승만과 무쵸 대사 사이에 대화가 있었을 수는 있겠습니다.

이 주제에서 더 충격적인 이야기는 미국 주도의 "유엔사"가 해롤드 J. 노블(Harold J. Noble)의 개인서신에서 "비실비실하는 늙은 바보"라고 불렸던 이승만을 제거하기 위해 "에버레디 작전"이라는 비밀 비상계획을 준비했다는 것입니다. 기밀해제된 문서에 따르면 원래의 계획은 합참의 지휘 하에 "유엔사" 겸 극동사령부사령관인 클라크(Mark W. Clark)장군이 1952년 7월에 초안을 작성했습니다. 당시 미국 관리들은 이승만 대통령의 "강압적 정책이 사회 불안을 불러일으키고 전쟁 노력을 훼손시킬 수 있다"고 우려했습니다.

필요시 이승만 체포와 "유엔사" 군정 수립을 포함하는 계획은, 이승만이 억류된 야당지도자들을 미국의 압력 하에 석방했기 때문에 실행되진 않았습니다. "유엔사"는 또한 1953년 5월 이승만이 정전협정 협상에 반대하고 "유엔사"에서 한국군을 철수하겠다고 위협했을 때 이 계획에 대해 또 다른 심각한 고려를 했습니다. 이승만을 달래기 위해 아이젠하워 대통령은 한국군을 "유엔사"의 통제 하에 계속 두도록 이승만에게 요청하는 한편 한국과의 안보조약 서명에 동의해야 했습니다.⁴

불행하게도 미국 정부는 오늘날까지 한국군으로의 전시작전통제권 환수를 지연·거부하고 있습니다. 70년 동안 미국 정부가 한국군을 군사적으

---

3 Omar N. Bradley and Clay Blair, *A General's Life*, (Touchstone, 1983), p.543
4 "Papers Show U.S. Considered Ousting Rhee in Korean War," *The NYT*, August 4, 1975

로 통제한다는 것은 사실상 자신의 군사 문제를 결정할 수 있는 한국 국민의 주권을 심각하게 침해한 것입니다.

2. 북한 침략과 점령

1950년 9월 15일 인천에 70,000여명의 병력이 성공적으로 상륙한 후 미국 주도의 "유엔사"는 서울을 탈환하고 남과 북을 가르는 38선을 향해 계속 진격했습니다. 9월 27일 합참은 맥아더에게 새로운 군사목표인 "북한군대의 파괴"를 위해 분단선을 넘도록 승인했습니다.[5] 10월 1일 국군 제1군단은 "선을 넘어 원산으로 진격했습니다."[6]

같은 날 도쿄에서 맥아더 장군은 "북한군"에게 항복하라는 요구를 발표했습니다. 이 메시지는 뉴욕, 유엔 미국대표부에 의해 '주한유엔군통합사

38선 돌파 후 찍은 기념사진

---

5 Callum A. MacDonald, *Korea: the War Before Vietnam*, (New York: Free Press, 1986), p.49
6 Wada Haruki, *The Korean War: An International History*, (Lanham, MD: Rowman and Littlefield, 2014), p.126

령부 특별보고'로 유엔에 전달됐습니다. 이 보고서에서 맥아더의 직함을 "통합사령부총사령관" 및 "유엔최고사령관"으로 기술했음에 주목하면 매우 흥미롭습니다. 또한 통합사령부는 구체적으로 "주한유엔군"이라고 언급했으며, 메시지에는 "유엔사령부"라는 명칭도 거론됐습니다.[7] 이 문서는 미국 정부가 통합사령부와 "유엔사"를 동일한 실체로 간주했다는 분명한 증거를 제공합니다.

어쨌든 북한을 침공함으로써 트루먼 행정부는 한국 사태를 다룬 두 개의 안보리결의의 약정을 위반했습니다.

안보리결의 83호 및 84호에 따라 유엔회원국은 "…한국에 무력 공격을 격퇴하고 해당 지역의 국제평화와 안보를 회복하는 데 필요한 지원을 제공…"하는데만 한국에서 무력을 사용하도록 허가되었습니다.

안보리결의 82호의 초기 요청인 "적대행위 중단" 과 "38선까지" 북한군의 철수를 고려할 때 "무력공격을 격퇴"한다는 의미는 북한군을 38도선으로 밀어내고 나서 가능한 한 정전협정을 체결하는 것이었음이 분명합니다. 미국 관리들 또한 처음에 이 목표를 공개·비공개적으로 확인했습니다. 6월 29일 애치슨은 미군이 '침략 이전의 상태로 대한민국을 회복하기 위한 목적으로만' 싸우고 있다고 선언했습니다.[8]

그러나 7월 중순부터 트루먼 행정부 내에서 북한 영토를 침공해 점령하자는 생각이 돌기 시작했습니다. 7월 13일 맥아더 장군은 도쿄를 방문한 두 명의 국방부장군에게 자신이 "북한군을…파괴하기 위해, 나는 북한 전체 점령이 필요할 수도 있다"고 말했습니다.[9]

---

7 S/1829, 1950년 10월 1일
8 Joseph C. Goulden, *Korea: The Untold Story of the War*, (McGraw-Hill Companies, 1983), p.237

맥아더의 견해는 북진통일론으로 무장한 반공십자군 이승만의 강한 야망을 지지하려는 그의 열망을 분명히 반영했습니다. 트루먼은 또한 7월 17일에 같은 문제에 대한 연구를 국가안보위원회(NSC)에 요청하여 '한국에 대한 미국의 조치절차' 보고서[10]가 그에게 제출되었습니다.

트루먼은 9월 11일 한국에서 새로운 미국의 목표를 제시한 보고서를 승인했습니다. "현재 한국에서의 유엔 조치가 소련이나 중국 공산주의자들과의 전면전 위험을 실질적으로 증가시키지 않으면서 이 정치적 목표(대한민국 하 통일정부 수립)를 달성할 수 있다면, 그 결과를 위해 <u>유엔 조치 압박을 옹호하는</u> 우리에게 이익이 될 것이다."[11]
보고서는 또한 합참에 "북한 점령 가능성에 대한 계획을 세우도록 주한 유엔군사령관에 대한 지휘"[12]를 인가하도록 권고했습니다.

이 보고서에서 특별히 주목되는 것은 "대한민국 하 통일한국"과 같은 다른 목표를 달성하기 위해 "이 임무(북한군을 38선으로 밀어냄) 수행을 넘어서는 38선 이북에서의 군사조치"는 "<u>현 안보리결의에 의해 분명히 승인된 바 없다</u>"는 것을 솔직히 인정하고 있는 것입니다. 따라서 보고서는 "이 정치적 목표를 추진하기 위해 군사조치를 위한 유엔승인"[13]을 새로 받아야 할 필요성이 있다고 결론지었습니다.

그러나 미국 정부는 소련 대표가 이미 1950년 8월 1일 안보리회의에 돌아왔기 때문에 안보리에서 소련의 거부권행사 가능성을 우려한 것 같습니다. 따라서 트루먼 행정부는 이 문제를 총회에 제출하기로 결정하고 워싱

---

9 Goulden, p.234
10 NSC-81/1, 1950년 9월 9일
11 NSC-81/1, p.1
12 NSC-81/1, p.4
13 NSC-81/1, p.3, Paragraph 12

턴에서 이미 결정된 통합사령부의 새로운 목표인 북한 영토를 점령하고 통일된 '대한민국 정부' 수립을 승인하는 결의안을 영국대표부와 작성했습니다. 외양을 위해 미국은 다시 영국과 다른 동맹국들에게 결의안의 공동후원을 요청했습니다.

북한 정부 대표에 대한 총회 참석 초대를 다시 거부 한 후 - 한국정부 대표는 초청하면서 - 미국이 지배하는 총회는 쉽게 1950년 10월 7일, '한국독립문제'라는 제목 하에 친미 공동결의안을 채택했는데 투표결과는 47(찬성) - 5(반대) - 7(기권)이었습니다. (참고.11, A/RES/376(5), **14** 1950년 10월 7일)

결의안 제목은 38선을 넘고 군사적 수단으로 북한을 점령하는 것에 대한 언급이 없었기 때문에 상당히 오해의 소지가 있었습니다. 그럼에도 불구하고 이 문제는 "한국전역의 안정상태를 보장하기 위해 모든 적절한 조치를 취한다"(1a), "유엔의 후원 하에" 선거를 실시함으로써 "한국의 주권 하에 통일되고 독립적이며 민주적인 정부를 수립한다"(1b), 그리고 "유엔군"은 "위에…명시된 목표를 달성"할 때까지만 "한국의 모든 곳에서 주둔한다"(1d)는 권고에 의해, 여러 해석을 가능케 하는 모호한 단어로 표현되었습니다.

또한 결의안은 총회에 두 개의 보조기구를 만들었습니다. 1) "전 한국(조선)의 통일된…정부수립을 위해" 유엔을 대표하는 "유엔한국통일부흥위원회(UNCURK)", 그리고 2) UNCURK가 "한국에 도착"할 때까지 "유엔통합사령부와 협의하고 자문하기 위한 (UNCURK의) 임시위원회"입니다.

트루먼 행정부는 10월 7일 총회 결의를 통해 북한에 대한 침략과 점령을

---

14 A/RES/376(5). A는 Assembly의 약자로 유엔총회를 의미합니다. A/RES/는 총회결의번호를 나타내는 형식입니다.

VII

RESOLUTIONS ADOPTED ON THE REPORTS OF THE FIRST COMMITTEE

376 (V). The problem of the independence of Korea

The General Assembly,

Having regard to its resolutions of 14 November 1947 (112 (II)), of 12 December 1948 (195 (III)) and of 21 October 1949 (293 (IV)),

Having received and considered the report[1] of the United Nations Commission on Korea,

Mindful of the fact that the objectives set forth in the resolutions referred to above have not been fully accomplished and, in particular, that the unification of Korea has not yet been achieved, and that an attempt has been made by an armed attack from North Korea to extinguish by force the Government of the Republic of Korea,

Recalling the General Assembly declaration of 12 December 1948 that there has been established a lawful government (the Government of the Republic of Korea) having effective control and jurisdiction over that part of Korea where the United Nations Temporary Commission on Korea was able to observe and consult and in which the great majority of the people of Korea reside; that this government is based on elections which were a valid expression of the free will of the electorate of that part of Korea and which were observed by the Temporary Commission; and that this is the only such government in Korea,

Having in mind that United Nations armed forces are at present operating in Korea in accordance with the recommendations[2] of the Security Council of 27 June 1950, subsequent to its resolution[3] of 25 June 1950, that Members of the United Nations furnish such assistance to the Republic of Korea as may be necessary to repel the armed attack and to restore international peace and security in the area,

Recalling that the essential objective of the resolutions of the General Assembly referred to above was the establishment of a unified, independent and democratic Government of Korea,

1. *Recommends that*

(*a*) All appropriate steps be taken to ensure conditions of stability throughout Korea;

(*b*) All constituent acts be taken, including the holding of elections, under the auspices of the United Nations, for the establishment of a unified, independent and democratic government in the sovereign State of Korea;

(*c*) All sections and representative bodies of the population of Korea, South and North, be invited to co-operate with the organs of the United Nations in the restoration of peace, in the holding of elections and in the establishment of a unified government;

(*d*) United Nations forces should not remain in any part of Korea otherwise than so far as necessary for achieving the objectives specified in sub-paragraphs (*a*) and (*b*) above;

(*e*) All necessary measures be taken to accomplish the economic rehabilitation of Korea;

2. *Resolves* that

(*a*) A Commission consisting of Australia, Chile, Netherlands, Pakistan, Philippines, Thailand and Turkey, to be known as the United Nations Commission for the Unification and Rehabilitation of Korea, be established to (i) assume the functions hitherto exercised by the present United Nations Commission on Korea; (ii) represent the United Nations in bringing about the establishment of a unified, independent and democratic government of all Korea; (iii) exercise such responsibilities in connexion with relief and rehabilitation in Korea as may be determined by the General Assembly after receiving the recommendations of the Economic and Social Council. The United Nations Commission for the Unification and Rehabilitation of Korea should proceed to Korea and begin to carry out its functions as soon as possible;

(*b*) Pending the arrival in Korea of the United Nations Commission for the Unification and Rehabilitation of Korea, the governments of the States represented on the Commission should form an Interim Committee composed of representatives meeting at the seat of the United Nations to consult with and advise the United Nations Unified Command in the light of the above recommendations; the Interim Committee should begin to function immediately upon the approval of the present resolution by the General Assembly;

(*c*) The Commission shall render a report to the next regular session of the General Assembly and to any prior special session which might be called to consider the subject-matter of the present resolution, and shall render such interim reports as it may deem appropriate to the Secretary-General for transmission to Members;

The General Assembly furthermore,

Mindful of the fact that at the end of the present hostilities the task of rehabilitating the Korean economy will be of great magnitude,

---
[1] See *Official Records of the General Assembly, Fifth Session, Supplement No. 16.*
[2] See *Official Records of the Security Council, Fifth Year,* No. 16.
[3] *Ibid.,* No. 15.

참고 11. A-Res-376(5) THE PROBLEM OF THE INDEPENDENCE OF KOREA, 1950.10.7 1951.1.1

무화과 잎으로 능숙하게 가릴 수 있었지만 그러한 결의가 분단된 조국의 평화적 재통일을 포함한 정치적 미래에 대한 한국(조선) 민중의 "자결권"(헌장 제1조 2항)을 심각하게 침해하여 채택되었다는 사실을 부정할 수는 없습니다.

미국은 무력으로 북한 인민에게 친미·친한 정부를 강요하기 위해 유엔 체제를 남용할 수 없습니다. 그러한 모호한 결의안은 유엔회원국들에 구속력이 없으며 헌장 제12조 1항, 제11조 2항, 제24조, 제25조 등을 노골적으로 위반함으로써 유엔헌장도 크게 훼손했습니다.

특히, 헌장 제12조 1항은 안보리가 "어떤 분쟁이나 사태"와 관련하여 부여된 기능을 행사하고 있는" 동안 총회가 그러한 분쟁이나 사태에 대해서 "어떤 권고를" 하는 것을 금지하고 있습니다.

안보리가 1950년 6월 25일부터 한국의 무력 충돌을 다루고 있었기 때문에, 총회가 위와 같은 조치를 권고한 10월 7일 결의를 채택했을 때 총회는 헌장 12(1)조를 위반하였습니다.

"유엔사" 병력에 의한 38선 통과는 중국 및 러시아로 한국 분쟁을 확대할 위험이 높기 때문에 유엔에 의한 이러한 위험한 군사기동에 대한 승인은, 우선 "국제평화와 안보의 유지에 대한 일차적 책임이 있는" 안보리의 승인을 받아야 했습니다. 사실 한국 문제는 1951년 1월 31일 결의 채택에 의해 공식적으로 제거될 때까지 안보리의 의제로 남아 있었습니다.[15]

언커크임시위원회(IC)의 역할은 10월 12일 결의 채택에서 그 실제 목적이 밝혀졌습니다. 이 결정의 핵심 부분은 4항, 언커크(UNCURK)의 추가 검토가 있을 때까지 "통합사령부가 현재 유엔군의 점령 하에 들어오는… 한국 지역에 대한 통치와 민사행정에 대한 모든 책임을 잠정적으로 맡도록 조언한다"[16]입니다.

달리 말하면 언커크임시위원회는 북한에 군정을 세울 수 있도록 "유엔

---

15 S/1995

16 A/1881, p.13

사"에 권한을 부여한 것입니다. 안보리가 당시 한국에서 무력 충돌을 처리하기 위한 관할권을 행사하고 있었기 때문에 이 임시위원회 결의도 무효입니다. 요컨대 총회가 "유엔사"의 외국군에게 조선민주주의인민공화국에 대한 침략, 북한 영토 점령, 군정 수립의 위임을 권고하는 것은 불법이었습니다.

불법적인 임시위원회 결의에 기초하여, "유엔사"는 북한 영토의 대부분을 점령한 1950년 10월과 11월 두 달 동안, 북한의 마을과 도시에 유엔군정을 수립했습니다. 동시에 이승만 정권의 군, 경찰, 반공청년단이 같은 지역에 독자적인 점령정부를 설치하고 있었습니다. 때로는 "미군방첩대조가 한국 경찰, 청년단과 함께 조선노동당 당원 명단에 있는 사람들을 개인적으로 색출하여 모아놓고" 많은 만행을 저질렀습니다.17

1953년 7월 정전협정에 서명한 후, "유엔사"는 이전 북한 영토 - 비무장지대 이남이지만 과거에 38선 이북 지역 - 에 거주하던 약 13,000명이 넘는 북한 인민들을 남한군대로 군정을 수립하여 통치했습니다.

이 지역을 이양해달라는 끊임없는 요구를 받은 후에야 "유엔사"는 마침내 1954년 11월 17일 한국 정부에게 이 지역에 대한 "행정권 이양"만을 합의했습니다.18 38선 이북, 군사분계선 이남지역에 대한 법적 관할권을 유지함으로써 "유엔사"는 대한민국 정부의 주권을 침해했습니다.

38선 이북 "수복지구"에 대한 행정권 이양식. 1954.11.17

---

17 Bruce Cumings, *The Korean War: A History*, (Modern Library, 2010), pp.196-197
18 한모니까, 「유엔군사령부의 '수복지구' 점령정책과 행정권이양(1950~54)」, 『역사비평』통권85호, 2008년 겨울호, (2008.11), p.3

3. 남북 협력사업 방해

최근 주한 "유엔사"는 남북 평화와 발전을 위한 협력사업을 승인하거나 차단하는 규제기관으로서의 새로운 역할을 불법적으로 행사하고 있습니다. 예를 들어, 2018년 8월 "유엔사"사령관은 북한의 철로 상태에 대한 남북 공동조사를 위해 남한 철도차량이 북한을 방문하는 것을 불허했습니다. 거부에 대한 변명은 한국 정부가 제출한 서류가 "불충분하다"는 것이었습니다. 이와 동시에 신문 보도는 남한이 북한의 개성에 열기 원했던 남북연락사무소 개설에 대해 미국이 "국경을 넘어 장비와 물자를 반입하면 유엔 제재를 위반할 수 있다는 불평"으로 간섭했다고 지적했습니다.[19]

또 다른 모욕적인 사건은 2018년 9월 25일, 차기 "유엔사"사령관, 한미연합사령관, 주한미군사령관으로 로버트 에이브럼스 장군을 지명한 미 상원군사위원회 청문회에서 발생했습니다. 2021년 7월 2일까지 "주한유엔사령관"을 지낸 에이브럼스 장군은 2018년 9월 19일 남북 합의에 대해 다음과 같이 언급했습니다.

> "그들이 (시작된)대화를 계속하겠지만, 그 모든 것이 유엔사에 의해 중개되고, 판결되고, 관찰되고, 집행되어야 한다."

달리 말하면, 한국 관리들이 경제 또는 군사협정에 서명할 수 있지만 "유엔사"의 검토와 승인을 받아야 한다는 것입니다. 이는 남북 협력문제에 대해 한국 주권을 인정치 않는다는 의미가 아니고 무엇입니까?

사실 미국의 한국정책 결정자는 미군 장성이 아닙니다. 남북 협정의 승인 여부를 최종 결정하는 것은 워싱턴 관리들입니다. 그러나 "유엔사"를 이

---

[19] 「주한미군 고위급 북한철도조사 차단」, 『조선일보』, 2018년 8월 31일

용한 미국의 내정 간섭은 유엔헌장 제2조 "평등권과 민족자결권의 원칙에 대한 존중에 기반하여 국가 간 우호관계를 발전시키려는 것"과 제3조 "모두를 위한 인권과 기본적 자유에 대한 존중을 증진하고 장려한다"는 유엔헌장의 주된 목적을 위반했습니다. 한국민은 남북한 거주 여부에 관계없이 기본적 인권과 발전, 평화, 여행, 결사 등의 자유를 향유할 자격이 있습니다. 어떤 외국 정부나 국제기구도 천 년 이상 통일된 나라로 함께 살아온 한국민의 이러한 자유를 제약할 수 없습니다.

더욱이 "유엔사"의 남북 관계 간섭은 안보리결의 83호 및 84호의 원래 임무를 위반하는 것이 됩니다. 이들 결의는 현재 조선민주주의인민공화국의 핵에 대한 유엔 제재와 아무런 관련이 없습니다.

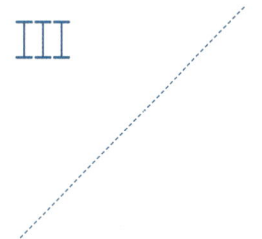

"유엔사"는 미국법을 위반하여 창설되었다

1. 유엔참여법 위반

미국이 유엔헌장을 국제조약으로 비준한 후, 1945년 8월 8일 첫 번째 유엔 창설 회원국이 되자 미국 의회는 곧 유엔 체계에 미국의 실질적인 참여를 승인하고 통제하기 위한 이행법을 통과시켰습니다. 유엔참여법(UNPA)으로 알려진 이 새로운 법률은 1945년 12월 20일에 발효되었습니다. 유엔참여법 6항[1]은 유엔안전보장이사회의 요청에 따라 미군을 제공하는 절차를 구체적으로 다루었습니다. 유엔헌장 제43조는 안보리의 요청에 따라 유엔의 모든 회원국에게 제공될 "군대의 수와 유형 및 지원"과 관련하여 안보리와 "특별협정"을 체결할 의무를 부과했습니다. 따라서 유엔참여법 제6항의 해당 부분은 다음과 같이 기술하고 있습니다.

> "대통령은 <u>헌장 43조에 따라 국제평화와 안보를 유지할 목적으로 안보리가 요청할 경우</u> 제공하는 <u>군대의 수와 유형</u>, 태세정도와 전체위치 및 통과권을 포함한 시설 및 지원의 성격에 대해, <u>적절한 법 또는 공동결의에 의해 의회의 승인을 받아야 하는</u> 특별협정 또는 협정을, 안보리와 협상할 권한이 있다."[2]

---

[1] 22 U.S.Code §287d

유엔참여법의 6절은 유엔 군사조치에의 미국 참여는 안보리와 자원하는 유엔회원국 간 "특별협정"이 우선 요구된다는 것을 미국 의회가 분명히 이해하였음을 보여줍니다. 그리고 미국에 대한 그러한 협정은 하원과 상원 모두의 승인을 필요로 했습니다. 그러나 트루먼 대통령과 그의 고문들은 분명히 이러한 법적 요건을 무시하기로 결정한 것 같습니다.

앞서 지적한 바와 같이 미국방부는 안보리의 지휘 아래로 미군을 예속시키려 하지 않았습니다. 또한 행정부 관리들은 그들의 결정에 대한 의회로부터의 질문이나 청문회를 피하고자 했습니다. 예를 들어 애치슨 국무장관은 "의원들의 공격 가능성이나 한국전쟁에의 군사개입에 대한 궁극적인 비용 또는 결과에 대해 전반적인 토론을 촉발시켜" 행정부의 "결정이 위험에 노출되는 것을 원치 않았다"는 것입니다.[3]

따라서 국무부와 국방부 관리들은 한국에서의 유엔 군사조치에 대한 안보리의 통제를 회피하고, 안보리와 특별협정을 맺을 필요가 없도록 하는 정도로 안보리결의 83호의 초안을 작성했습니다. 이것은 트루먼 행정부가 유엔헌장 42조와 43조의 요구사항을 무시한다는 것을 의미했습니다. 그 과정에서 행정부 관리들은 유엔참여법의 요구사항, 특히 유엔의 군사 강제조치에 있어 미군 참여를 위해 마련된 특정 절차를 따르지 않았습니다.

그럼에도 불구하고 트루먼과 그의 참모들은 그들의 진짜 의도를 숨기고, 유엔의 이름으로 또는 유엔의 "경찰조치"로, 한국에서의 군사조치를 정당화하려고 했습니다. 예를 들어, 1950년 6월 25일 저녁(미국 동부시간) 블레어하우스의 첫 번째 고위관리회의에서 브래들리 장군(합참의장)은 참가자들에게 "우리는 유엔에 대한 <u>원조라고 위장하여</u> 행동해야 합니다."

---

[2] 22 U.S.C §287d
[3] Glenn D. Paige, *The Korean Decision, June 24-30, 1950*, (Free Press, 1968), p.187

라고 조언했고 트루먼 대통령은 "우리는 유엔을 위해 전적으로 일하고 있다"고 강조했습니다.[4]

또한, 트루먼은 1950년 6월 29일 기자회견에서 자신의 행동을 유엔의 "경찰조치"라고 묘사함으로써 한국에 대한 미군의 개입사실을 최소화하려고 했습니다. 이는 거짓말이었는데, 왜냐하면 트루먼은 6월 26일 밤 블레어하우스 2차 회의에서 이미 미 공군과 해군에게 남한군에 대한 "전면적 지원"을 명령함으로써 조선민주주의인민공화국의 인민군에 대항한 주요 군사조치를 이미 승인했기 때문입니다.[5]

2. 미국 헌법 위반

대통령이 미군의 "총사령관"직을 수행하지만 "전쟁 선포"의 실질적인 권한은 미국 헌법 제1조 8절 11항에 따라 의회에 있습니다. 과거 역사에서 대통령은 때때로 미국인의 생명을 구하거나 미국 국익을 보호하기 위해, 공식적인 전쟁 선포나 의회의 승인없이 해외에서의 소규모 전투 개입에 미국 군함이나 군대를 사용했었습니다.

그러나 주요 전쟁에서, 대통령은 제1조 8절에 따라 전쟁 시작 전이나 직후에 의회로부터 공식적 전쟁 선포를 받도록 요구되었습니다. 미국 의회가 공식적으로 전쟁 선포를 채택한 5개의 전쟁이 있었습니다. 즉, 1812년 전쟁, 멕시코-미국전쟁, 스페인-미국전쟁, 제1차 세계대전, 제2차 세계대전입니다.

---

[4] *FRUS*, 1950, Korea, Volume VII, Doc. 86
[5] Dean Acheson, *Present at the Creation*, (W.W. Norton, 1969), p.407

한국 분쟁이 전쟁인지 아닌지 여부는 미국 법원에서 엇갈렸지만, 미국 최고군사법원은 한국사태전을 다루면서 명확하고 강력한 의견을 내놓는 것을 주저하지 않았습니다. 미국 대 밴크로프트 사건6에서 미국 군사항소법원은 다음과 같이 발표했습니다.

> "한국의 분쟁에 대한 일간신문 기사 독해, 관련된 군대의 규모에 대한 이해, 해당 지역에서 군사작전을 유지하기 위해 사용되는 군대 및 민간인 노력에 대한 인식, 그리고 다른 잘 알려진 전시활동에 대한 지식은 우리가 <u>고도로 심화된 전쟁상태에 있다는 것을 조금도 의심할 여지없이 우리에게 확신시켜 줍니다</u>."7

미군 사상자와 전쟁비용만 계산해도 한국전쟁은 사실상 미국 전체 전쟁 중 5위를 차지합니다. 한국에서의 미군 사상자만 약 130,000명이었습니다. 그리고 미국의 전쟁비용은 1950~1953년 기간만 계산하면, 2019년 달러로 약 3,900억 달러였습니다.8

한국전쟁은 미국의 주요 전쟁이었기 때문에 트루먼 대통령은 미국 헌법에 따라 의회에 조선민주주의인민공화국(북한)과 중화인민공화국(중국)에 대한 선전포고를 채택하도록 요청할 법적 의무가 있었습니다. 그의 행정부가 유엔헌장 제42조와 제43조와 유엔참여법 6조에 따라 행동하지 않았기 때문에 그는 특히 이 조치를 취해야했습니다.

더욱이 안보리결의 83호가 법적으로 유효하다고 가정하더라도 그 권고는 유엔 조치가 아니기에 미국 정부를 구속하지 않았습니다. 한국 내전에

---

6 U.S. v. Bancroft, 3 C.M.A. 3, 11 C.M.R. 3, 3 U.S.C.M.A. 3(1953) July 3, 1953 · US Court of Military Appeals · No.1139

7 George W. Latimer 판사의 의견, 다른 2명의 판사가 동의함.

8 「전쟁에서의 미국군사상자」, Wikipedia, 2021년 6월 7일 검색, 「미국 역사상 가장 비싼 전쟁」, 24/7 *Wallst*, 2019년 6월 7일

참전할지 말지 여부에 대한 결정은 유엔회원국 각자에게 달린 것이었습니다. 조선민주주의인민공화국과의 전쟁수행결정권은 분명히 미국 의회에 속했지 대통령에 속하지 않았습니다. 그러나 트루먼은 1950년 6월 27일과 30일 백악관에서 미 의회의 주요 지도자들에게 이미 한국에서 미군을 사용하기로 한 결정에 대해 두 차례의 짧은 브리핑을 했을 뿐 의회에 공식적인 선전포고를 요청한 적이 없었습니다. 이는 미국 헌법에 대한 명백한 위반이었습니다.

트루먼의 일방적인 행동에 대한 반응으로 국회의원 대부분은 매카시즘에 대한 두려움 때문에 침묵을 유지했습니다. 그럼에도 불구하고 의회에서 트루먼의 행동을 공개적으로 비판한 몇몇 용감한 의원들이 있었습니다. 그 중에는 태프트(Robert A. Taft) 상원의원(오하이오 주), 웨리(Kenneth S. Wherry) 상원의원(네브래스카 주), 마르칸토니오(Vito Marcantonio) 하원의원(미국 노동당-NY)이 있었습니다.

태프트 상원의원은 "대통령이 '의회 승인 없이 한국에 개입하면 말레이시아나 인도네시아, 이란, 남미에서 전쟁을 할 수 있다'고 경고했습니다."[9]

하원에서 마르칸토니오 의원은 다음과 같이 선언했습니다. "우리가 유엔헌장에 합의했을 때 우리는 유엔헌장을 우리 헌법으로 대신하는데 합의하지 않았습니다. 전쟁을 선포하고 실행할 수 있는 권한은 미국 의회에 있는 국민의 대표들에게 있습니다."[10] 미국 조약이 그 땅의 최고법인 미국 헌법을 대체할 수 없다는 의원의 성명은 옳은 것입니다.[11]

---

[9] Louis Fisher, "The Korean War: On What Legal Basis Did Truman Act?," The American Journal of International Law, Vol. 89:21, 1995, p.35

[10] Ibid.

[11] Reid v. Covert, 354 U.S. 1, 17 (1956) 참조

불행하게도 태프트 상원의원이 예언적으로 경고한 것처럼 트루먼의 한국에서의 일방적인 전쟁은 이후 수십 년 동안 전쟁에 대한 의회의 권력을 약화시키는 데 치명적인 영향을 미쳤으며, 그의 나쁜 선례를 이어 존슨의 베트남, 캄보디아, 라오스, 클린턴의 유고슬라비아, 오바마의 리비아처럼 다른 미국 대통령들도 트루먼의 뒤를 따랐기에, 그 후부터 전쟁에 대한 의회의 권력을 약화시키는 데 치명적인 영향을 미쳤습니다.

IV. "유엔사"는 일본 평화헌법을 위반했다

1. 헌법 9조 '전쟁능력' 금지의 위반

제2차 세계대전 이후 일본의 헌법은 1946년 11월 3일 국회에서 처음 제정되어 1947년 5월 3일에 발효되었습니다. 국가정책으로서 전쟁을 포기하는 조항 때문에 세계적으로 유명해졌습니다. 이 헌법 제9조는 다음과 같이 밝히고 있습니다.

> "1. 일본 국민은 정의와 질서에 기초한 국제평화를 진심으로 염원하며, 국가의 주권으로서의 전쟁과 국제분쟁 해결의 수단으로서의 무력의 위협 또는 행사를 영원히 포기한다.
>
> 2. 전항의 목적을 달성하기 위하여 육해공군뿐만 아니라 기타 전력을 절대 유지하지 않는다. 국가의 교전권을 인정하지 아니한다."[1]

미국과 일본에서는 여전히 맥아더 장군이 9조의 초안을 작성했다고 오해하는 부분이 있지만, 현재 이 조항에 대한 진짜 공로는 1945년 10월 미군 점령당국에 의해 전후 일본 최초의 총리로 선출되었던 전 일본 외무대신 시데하라 키주로에게 있음이 확인됐습니다.[2]

---

[1] https://japan.kantei.go.jp/constitution_and_government_of_japan/constitution_e.html

맥아더는 제9조를 수호하는 대신에, 특히 한국전쟁 초기에 "전쟁능력"의 유지 또는 참전에 대한 9조의 법적 금지를 훼손하는데 있어서 핵심적 역할을 했습니다. 예를 들어, 1950년 7월 8일 그는 "일본 정부에 75,000명의 경찰예비대를 설치하고 해상보안대를 8,000명 증원할 것을 명령했습니다."[3] 당시 일본은 아직 미군의 점령 하에 있었기 때문에 요시다 행정부는 이 위헌적 명령을 따를 수밖에 없었습니다. 1950년 7월 13일, 맥아더는 도쿄사령부를 방문한 미합참 대표단에게 "일본 경찰력은 일본에 안보를 제공하기 위해 미국 장비를 갖춘 4개 사단의 보안대로 전환되어야 한다"고 말했습니다.[4]

그 후 일본 경찰예비대는 1952년 10월에 "보안대"로 개명되었고 1954년 7월에는 "자위대"로 다시 개명되었습니다. 이에 맥아더는 미극동사령부총사령관, 주일연합군최고사령관(SCAP), "유엔사"총사령관으로서 헌법 9조의 상비군 금지를 위반하며 일본이 다시 재무장하는 길을 닦았습니다.

오늘날 일본은 세계적 군사강국 중 하나로 인정받고 있습니다. 2020년 연간 군사비 지출은 490억 달러로 세계 9위입니다. 이에 비해 한국은 2020년에 460억 달러를 군비로 지출했습니다.[5] 일본의 공군력은 1,480대의 전투기로 세계 6위입니다. 해군은 155척의 군함을 보유하고 있으며, 육군은 약 1,000대의 탱크와 약 250,000명의 군인을 보유하고 있습니다.[6] 이런 종류의 군사력 강도는 분명히 "전쟁능력"에 해당하므로 일본 헌법 9조에 위배됩니다.

---

2 James E. Auer, "Article Nine of Japan's Constitution," *Law and Contemporary Problems*, Spring 1990, pp.173-174

3 Wada, p.93

4 J. Lawton Collins, *War in Peacetime: The History and Lessons of Korea*, (Boston: Houghton Mifflin Company, 1969), p.83

5 SIPRI 2020년 군사지출 참조

6 www.globalfirepower.com

2. 일본의 한국전쟁 참전

일본 헌법은 9조를 "전쟁 포기"라는 제목으로 별도의 "제2장"에 포함시켜 크게 강조하고 있습니다. 9조 첫 항은 일본 국민이 "민족의 주권으로서의 전쟁을 영원히 포기한다"고 명시하고 있습니다. 이 단락과 함께 일본의 전후 헌법에 9조가 포함된 이유를 이해하기 위해 헌법 전문을 읽는 것도 도움이 됩니다. 전문의 첫 번째 단락은 제2차 세계대전 중 태평양전쟁과 같은 또 다른 참혹한 전쟁을 피하기 위한 일본 국민의 강한 결의를 보여줍니다.

"우리는 정부의 행위로 다시는 전쟁의 참화가 일어나지 않도록 한다."

전문의 두 번째 약속은 "영원한 평화"에 대한 일본 국민의 염원입니다. 마지막 요점은 일본인이 평화와 안전을 달성하는 방법을 설명합니다. 그것은 다른 국민들의 "공포와 결핍에서 벗어나 평화롭게 살 권리"를 인정함으로써, "세계의 평화를 사랑하는 국민들의 공정과 신의"를 신뢰함으로써, 그리고 "모든 나라와 평화로운 협력"을 추구함으로써입니다.

따라서 일본은 9조를 유지하기 위해, 다른 군사강국과의 군사동맹을 피하고, 일본 영토가 다른 나라들의 군사기지로 사용되는 것을 거부하며, 모든 국가와 우호관계를 유지하는 것이 필수적입니다.

불행하게도 일본을 미국의 군사동맹국으로 만들기 위해 트루먼 행정부는 "일본에 압력을 가해 9조를 수정하고 빠르면 1948년에 재무장할 것을 요구"했습니다."[7]

---

[7] Umeda, Sayuri, "Japan: Interpretations of the Article 9 of the Constitution"(2015); www.loc.gov. 2021년 6월 16일 검색

특히, "미국인 카이사르"라고도 알려진 맥아더는 9조를 위반하여 일본을 한국 전쟁 주요참전국으로 전환하는데서 중심 역할을 했습니다. 무엇보다도 1950년 7월 도쿄에 "유엔사"의 군사령부를 설치하고 오키나와에 약 200개(현재 약 100개)의 미군기지를 운용했으며, 일본 본토는 한국전쟁을 수행하기 위한 병참기지로 활용했습니다. 일본은 또한 한국에 있는 북한군과 시설에 대한 미국의 항공 및 해상공격의 발사대가 되었습니다. 예를 들어, 미 극동공군 내의 3개 항공단 중 2개, 나고야의 5공군과 오키나와의 카데나 공군기지의 20공군은 일본으로부터 전진배치되었습니다.

1950년 6월 극동공군은 "F-80C 365대를 포함해 총 1,172대"를 보유했습니다.[8] 이 전투기와 폭격기는 이타주케, 요코타, 미사와, 카데나 등 일본의 여러 공군기지에 전개되어 있었습니다. 7월 16일 "카데나에서 온 47대의 항공기가 서울의 정렬된 철도조차장을 공격했습니다." "8월 중순 98대의 B-29가 요코타 공군기지와 카데나 공군기지로부터 비행임무를 수행하고 있었습니다."[9] 그러나 요시다 내각은 "전쟁에서 국가의 역할을 인정하지 않았고, 국민들도 그것을 모르고 있었습니다."[10]

한국전쟁에서 일본 역할의 전체 범위는 아직까지 일본과 미국 양국 정부가 그 역사를 상당 부분 비밀로 하고 있어 평가하기 어렵습니다. 한국전쟁에 참전한 일본 국민들은, 가용한 공개정보를 기반으로 하면 최소 5,000명입니다. 그들은 세 그룹으로 나눌 수 있습니다.

첫 번째 그룹은, "유엔사"가 1950년 9월 크로마이트 작전(인천상륙작전)에 유인·모집·동원한 "3,922명의 일본징발노동자들"입니다.[11] 이 일본인

---

8   Wada, pp.91-92
9   Wada, p.92
10 Wada, p.95

대원들은 "37척"의 LST(탱크상륙함)를 운항하여 "미 해병대 상륙부대의 79%"를 수송했습니다.[12]

두 번째 그룹은 "54명의 전 제국해군 장교"를 포함하여 "1,200"명의 해상안전위원회(MSB) 일본 정부직원으로 구성되었습니다. 맥아더 명령 하에 일본 정부는 1950년 가을 한국의 여러 항구에서, 미7함대의 기뢰제거작전을 위해 "총 54명의 소해대원"을 제공했습니다. 작전은 미군 상륙을 위한 바다 청소를 위해 "10월 10일 원산 일대"에서 시작됐습니다. 다른 작전은 "인천, 군산, 해주, 진남포"에서 수행되었습니다.[13]

세 번째 그룹은 1950년 주일 미군기지에서 일했거나, 미군을 따라 한국전쟁터까지 갔던 "약120명"의 일본 지원 노동자로 구성됐습니다. 이 그룹에는 요리사, 운전사, 통역사, 유지보수 노동자, 미군들에 의해 "하우스 보이"로 고용됐던 10대들이 포함됐습니다. 적은 인원이었지만 그들은 미군 제복을 입고 총을 들고 미군과 함께 북한이나 중국군에 맞서 싸우며 주한 미군부대의 일원이 됐습니다. 그들 중 일부는 전투에서 분명히 사망했으며 생존자들은 "1952년 중반"까지 미군에 의해 일본으로 송환되었으며, "북한에 있는 2명의 일본인 전쟁포로 중 1명은 1953년 8월에 귀국했습니다."[14]

전쟁 초기 6개월 동안 많은 일본인이 사망했습니다. "일본 특별조달청의 추산에 따르면 56명의 일본 선원과 노동자가 사망했습니다." "23명의 사망은 일본 소해함이 기뢰에 의해 침몰할 때 발생했습니다."[15]

---

11 Tessa Morris-Suzuki, "Post- War Warriors: Japanese Combatants in the Korean War," *The Asia-Pacific Journal*, Vol. 10, Issue 31, No. 1, July 30, 2012
12 Wada, p.113
13 Wada, pp.138-139
14 Morris-Suzuki, 위 글
15 Morris-Suzuki, 위 글

3. 허위 "유엔-일본정부 간 SOFA" 설정과 "유엔사" 병참기지화

1951년 9월 8일 일본과의 평화조약이 체결되었을 때 미 국무장관 딘 애치슨(Dean Acheson)은 일본 총리 요시다(Yoshida)로부터 다음과 같은 위임을 교환공문으로 받았습니다.

> "평화조약이 발효된 후 1개국 혹은 2개국 이상의 유엔회원국 군대가 극동에서의 유엔조치에 참여하는 경우, 일본은 그러한 유엔조치에 참여하는 회원국이나 회원국들의 군대를 일본 국내 및 그 부근에 주둔하는 것을 허용하고 용이하게 할 것이다."**16**

미국 정부는 이 공문에서 일본에 주둔하거나 통과하는 "유엔군"과 그 가족들의 법적 지위와 특권에 대해 "한국에서의 유엔조치"를 명분으로 세부적 합의를 받아냈습니다. 이에 따라 1954년 2월 19일 일본 정부는 통합사령부 역할을 하는 미국 정부와 8개의 "전력제공국"과 "주일유엔군의 지위에 관한 협정"에 서명했습니다.**17**

유엔 관리 누구도 이 협정에 서명하지 않았지만, "유엔사"는 이 협정을 마치 유엔과 일본 사이에 체결된 것처럼 위장하여 이 협정을 "유엔-일본정부 간 SOFA"라고 부릅니다.**18**

이 협정에서 또 다른 심각한 미국의 잘못된 표현은 "유엔군"이라는 용어의 사용입니다. 협정 제1조는 이를 "유엔 결의에 따른 조치를 위해 파견되는 파견국의 육해공군"이라고 정의하고 있습니다. "파견국"의 군대가 어떻게 "유엔군"이 되었습니까?

---

16 TIAS 2490

17 TIAS 2995

18 https://www.yokota.af.mil/Portals/44/Documents/Units/AFD-150924-004.pdf. 유엔사령부-후방 정보 시트

안보리가 유엔헌장 제42조와 제43조에 따라 유엔회원국으로부터 군대를 모으기로 결정했다면, 그러한 군대는 실제로 유엔군이라고 부를 수 있지만 1950년 한국에 파견된 외국 군대의 경우는 그렇지 않았습니다.

앞서 지적한 바와 같이 유엔 법무국은 1994년 한국에 파견된 외국군이 "걸프전에서 결성된 연합군과 유사"할 뿐 유엔과는 무관한 기구임을 분명히 했습니다. 1991년 걸프전 당시 쿠웨이트에서 이라크군을 추방하기 위해 사용한 연합군의 정식 명칭은 2003년 미국의 이라크 침공 및 점령의 경우처럼 "미국 주도 연합군" 또는 "미국 주도 다국적군"이었습니다.

미국은 걸프전에서 연합군 작전에 대한 안보리 승인을 획득했지만 조지 H. W 부시 대통령은 자기 이름으로 한국에서의 미국 주도 연합군을 "유엔사"라고 한 트루먼의 거짓말을 반복하진 않았습니다. 한국전과 걸프전 모두에서 미국 주도의 연합군은 유엔안보리의 지휘와 통제 하에 있지 않았습니다.

미국 주도 연합군이 일본에 주둔하거나 통과할 수 있는 특권을 얻는 것 외에도 "유엔-일본정부 간 SOFA"에는 두 가지 실제 목적이 있었던 것으로 보입니다.

첫째는, 1953년 7월 정전협정으로 한국에서의 전투가 중단된 후에도 '병참기지'로서 주일 미군기지를 확실히 장기간 무료 사용하기 위한 의도입니다.

둘째는, 만일 필요하다면 미래에 "이 협정에 서명하지 않은 모든 국가"가 언제든 가입할 수 있도록 허용함으로써, 만일 그러한 국가가 "1950년 6월 25일, 6월 27일 및 7월 7일 유엔 안보리 결의와 1951년 2월 1일 유엔총회 결의"를 지원하기 위해 한국에 군대를 파견할 의사가 있다면, 제22조에 따라 "유엔사"를 확장하기 위한 것입니다.

제24조와 제25조에 따르면 이 협정은 "모든 유엔군이 일본에서 철수"하거나 동일한 군대가 "한국에서 철수"한 후 90일 이내에 "종료한다"고 명시하고 있습니다. 이것은 "유엔사"가 일본에 미군이 아닌 "유엔사" 군인을 한 명만 유지한다면 이 조약이 무기한 계속된다는 것을 의미할까요? 요코타 공군기지에 있는 "유엔사-후방"사무실의 현재 관행에 비추어 볼 때 대답은 "예"인 것 같습니다.

2018년에는 요코타 공군기지에 위치한 "유엔사-후방" 사무실에는 사령관인 호주 공군장교, 부사령관은 캐나다 공군장교와 함께 오직 4명의 "유엔사" 병사만이 있었습니다. 요코타 외에 일본에 있는 6개의 다른 주일 미군기지도 미국 정부와 일본 정부에 의해 "유엔사" 기지로 지정되어 있습니다. 그것은 캠프 자마, 요코스카 미해군기지, 사세보 미해군기지, 카데나 미공군기지, 화이트 비치 미해군시설 및 후텐마 미해병대 기지입니다.

일본에 허위의 "유엔-일본정부 SOFA"를 부과함으로써 미국 주도 "유엔사"는 한국전쟁이 계속되는 동안, 그리고 "유엔사-후방"기지가 일본에 유지되는 동안, 일본이 또 다른 참혹한 전쟁에 휩싸일 가능성을 높임으로써, 그리고 일본 국민이 "영원한 평화"속에 사는 것을 불가능하게 만듦으로써, 일본 평화헌법 9조를 다시 위반했습니다.

앞으로 한국에서 전쟁이 다시 재개된다면 미국 정부는 일본 자위대를 "유엔사" 군대에 편입시켜 북한군에 맞서 싸우게 할 것이라는 점은 충분히 예상할 수 있습니다.

"유엔사" 해체는 오래 지연되었다

1. 유엔은 이미 "유엔사" 해체를 요청했다.

1975년은 1947년부터 진행된 유엔총회의 "한국 문제" 논의에서 역사적인 전환점이 되었습니다. 2차 세계대전 이후 식민지 권력으로부터 독립을 달성한 후 신생국들이 유엔에 가입하면서 유엔 내에서는 한민족의 자결권과 외국 간섭 없는 분단 한국의 평화통일을 지지해왔습니다. 이러한 긍정적인 추세는 마침내 1975년 "한국 문제"에 대한 총회 논의에 한반도의 양국 정부대표 초청으로 귀결되었습니다. 격렬한 논쟁 끝에 총회는 다소 혼란스러운 방식으로 한국에 대한 두 가지 다른 결의를 채택했습니다. 결의3390(xxx) A는 미국과 27개 동맹국이 공동후원한 초안을 기반으로 한 반면, 결의3390(xxx) B는 알제리 및 중화인민공화국을 포함한 43개 비동맹 및 사회주의 국가가 공동후원한 초안을 기반으로 했습니다.

흥미롭게도 두 결의는 이제 "유엔사령부" 해체 필요성과 남한에서 유엔깃발 하에 복무하는 모든 외국군을 철수해야한다는데 기본적인 합의를 이루었습니다. 그러나 미국이 후원한 결의는 "유엔사" 해체에 조건을 첨부했습니다. "직접 관계당사국들"이 대화를 시작하고 "정전협정 유지"를 위한 "새로운 합의"를 해야 한다는 것이었습니다. 한편 결의B는 그러한 조건 없이, 한국 정전협정을 "평화협정"으로 대체할 "정전협정의 실제 당사국"을 단지 요청했습니다.

특히 결의B는 "유엔사령부"라는 용어에 인용부호를 사용하여 유엔결의에서 처음으로 그 이름에 대한 비승인을 표시한 점이 주목되었습니다. (참고.12, A/RES/3390(XXX), 1975년 11월 18일)

결의B의 채택은 북한과 총회에서의 그 지지자들에겐 큰 승리였는데 그것은 결의B가 더 많은 공동발의자와 더 유리한 투표결과를 가지고 있었기 때문입니다. 54 (찬성) - 43 (반대) - 42 (기권).

바꿔 말하면, 기권표가 찬성표에 추가되었다면 투표회원국들 3분의 2 이상이 결의B를 지지한 것입니다(투표에서 기권한 사람들은 결의B를 지지하는 경향이 있었지만 미국 정부에 대한 두려움 때문에 공개적으로 이를 표명하기를 꺼려했습니다). 한국에 전투를 위해 군대를 파견한 일부 국가들조차 결의B를 지지하거나(에티오피아) 기권(그리스, 필리핀, 태국)했다는 점도 주목할 만합니다.

안타깝게도 미국, 북한, 한국, 중국 간에 두 결의의 후속조치를 위한 회담이 열리지 않았습니다. 총회 제1위원회가 결의B를 채택한 후, 북한 정부는 한국에서 "모든 외국군이 철수한다는 조건으로 미국과 평화협정을 체결하겠다"는 의지를 표명한 성명[1]을 발표했습니다.

한편 미국 정부는 미군이 남한에 남을 수 있도록 정전협정에서 "유엔사"의 임무를 한·미군에 할당하기 위한 회담에만 관심이 있었습니다. 미국 정부는 또한 한국 정부의 참여 없이 당시 평화협정을 논의할 의지가 없었습니다.

---

1   A/10354

apartheid, which remain the main obstacles to the strengthening of international peace and security,

Reaffirming the close link existing between the strengthening of international security, disarmament, decolonization, development and the need for a more intensive international effort to narrow the widening gap between the developed and the developing countries, and also stressing, in this connexion, the importance of the early implementation of the decisions adopted at its seventh special session,

Emphasizing the need constantly to strengthen the peace-keeping and peace-making role of the United Nations, as well as its role in promoting development through co-operation,

1. *Solemnly calls upon* all States to seek strict and consistent implementation of the purposes and principles of the Charter of the United Nations and of all the provisions of the Declaration on the Strengthening of International Security as a basis for relations among States, irrespective of their size, level of development and socio-economic system;

2. *Also calls upon* all States to extend the process of détente to all regions of the world, with the equal participation of all States, in order to bring about just and lasting solutions to international problems so that peace and security will be based on effective respect for the sovereignty and independence of all States and the inalienable rights of each people to determine its own destiny freely and without outside interference, coercion or pressure;

3. *Reaffirms* the legitimacy of the struggle of peoples under alien domination to achieve self-determination and independence and appeals to all States to implement the Declaration on the Granting of Independence to Colonial Countries and Peoples[11] and the other resolutions of the United Nations on the total elimination of colonialism, racism and *apartheid*;

4. *Reaffirms* that any measure or pressure directed against any State while exercising its sovereign right freely to dispose of its natural resources constitutes a flagrant violation of the right of self-determination of peoples and the principle of non-intervention, as set forth in the Charter, which, if pursued, could constitute a threat to international peace and security;

5. *Reaffirms* its opposition to any threats of use of force, intervention, aggression, foreign occupation and measures of political and economic coercion which attempt to violate the sovereignty, territorial integrity, independence and security of States,

6. *Recommends* urgent measures to stop the arms race and promote disarmament, including the convening of the World Disarmament Conference, the dismantling of foreign military bases, the creation of zones of peace and the encouragement of general and complete disarmament and strengthening of the United Nations, in order to eliminate the causes of international tensions and ensure international peace, security and co-operation;

7. *Takes note* of the report of the Secretary-General,[12] requests him to submit to the General Assembly at its thirty-first session a report on the implementation of the Declaration on the Strengthening of International Security and decides to include in the provisional agenda of its thirty-first session the item entitled "Implementation of the Declaration on the Strengthening of International Security".

2409th plenary meeting
18 November 1975

3390 (XXX). Question of Korea

A

The General Assembly,

Mindful of the hope expressed by it in resolution 3333 (XXIX) of 17 December 1974,

Desiring that progress be made towards the attainment of the goal of peaceful reunification of Korea on the basis of the freely expressed will of the Korean people,

Recalling its satisfaction with the issuance of the joint communiqué at Seoul and Pyongyang on 4 July 1972 and the declared intention of both the South and the North of Korea to continue the dialogue between them,

Further recalling that, by its resolution 711 A (VII) of 28 August 1953, the General Assembly noted with approval the Armistice Agreement of 27 July 1953,[13] and that, in its resolution 811 (IX) of 11 December 1954, it expressly took note of the provision of the Armistice Agreement which requires that the Agreement shall remain in effect until expressly superseded either by mutually acceptable amendments and additions or by provisions in an appropriate agreement for a peaceful settlement at a political level between both sides,

Aware, however, that tension in Korea has not been totally eliminated and that the Armistice Agreement remains indispensable to the maintenance of peace and security in the area,

Noting the letter of 27 June 1975,[14] addressed to the President of the Security Council by the Government of the United States of America, affirming that it is prepared to terminate the United Nations Command on 1 January 1976, provided that the other parties directly concerned reach agreement on alternative arrangements mutually acceptable to them for maintaining the Armistice Agreement,

Noting the statement of 27 June 1975 by the Government of the Republic of Korea affirming its willingness to enter into arrangements for maintaining the Armistice Agreement,

Recognizing that, in accordance with the purposes and principles of the Charter of the United Nations regarding the maintenance of international peace and security, the United Nations has a continuing responsibility to ensure the attainment of this goal on the Korean peninsula,

1. *Reaffirms* the wishes of its members, as expressed in the consensus statement adopted by the General Assembly on 28 November 1973,[15] and urges both the South and the North of Korea to continue their dialogue to expedite the peaceful reunification of Korea;

---

[11] Resolution 1514 (XV).
[12] A/10205 and Add.1.
[13] See *Official Records of the Security Council, Eighth Year, Supplement for July, August and September 1953*, document S/3079; transmitted to the members of the General Assembly by a note of the Secretary-General (A/2451).
[14] *Ibid., Thirtieth Year, Supplement for April, May and June 1975*, document S/11737.
[15] *Official Records of the General Assembly, Twenty-eighth Session, Supplement No. 30* (A/9030), p. 24, item 41.

참고 12. A-RES-3390(XXX), 한국문제 1975.11.18

반면 조선민주주의인민공화국 정부는 대한민국 정부의 평화회담 참여를 허용할 의사가 없었는데, 이는 한국이 1953년 정전협정 체결을 최종적으로 거부했고, 게다가 한국군이 미군 작전통제 하에 있었기 때문입니다.

그럼에도 불구하고 북한은 1997년 한반도 평화협정을 위한 4자회담에 동의 한 이래 한국 정부의 평화회담 참여를 개방해 왔습니다. 안타깝게도 미국이 평화협정을 체결한 후에도 남한에서의 미군철수 거부 의견을 고집하고 있기 때문에 이러한 회담은 성공하지 못했습니다.

2. "유엔사"는 1978년부터 허울뿐인 집단이다.

1953년 한국전쟁 정전협정 체결 후 "유엔사"16개국은 한국에서 군대를 철수하기 시작했고, 미군을 제외한 대부분의 외국 군대는 1970년대 초반에 고국으로 복귀했습니다. 1975년에도 여전히 한국에는 약 4만 명의 미군이 있었습니다. 그러나 한 미국 대표는 1975년 11월 유엔총회 대표들에게 "유엔사"에는 "300명 미만"의 미군이 있고 나머지 미군은 "양자협정"(1953년 한미상호방위조약)에 따라 한국에 주둔하고 있다고 깜짝 발표했습니다.

"유엔사" 해체에 대한 총회에서의 요구가 증가함에 따라 미국은 한국군이라도 작전통제할 한미 군사구조를 만들고자 했습니다. 그리하여 1978년 11월 7일 "유엔사"와 함께 한미연합군을 지휘하는 "한미연합사령부"라는 새로운 군사조직이 창설되었습니다. 이때 한국 정부는 "한국군에 대한 "유엔사"의 작전통제권을 연합사에" 위임했습니다. 때문에 한국군은 "유엔사"로부터 연합사 통제로 이동했지만 미군은 이에 따르지 않았습니다.[2]

---

[2] Col. Shawn P. Creamer, U.S. Army, "The United Nations Command and The Sending States," *International Journal of Korean Studies*, Vol. XXI, No. 2, Fall-Winter 2017, p.14

그러나 1994년 한국 정부는 연합사로부터 한국군의 평시작전통제권을 되찾아왔습니다. 현재 연합사의 주요 역할은 평시에 한미연합전쟁연습을 계획하고 통제하는 것입니다. 그러나 적대행위가 발생하면, 한미연합사는 "양국의 모든 복무 중인 600,000명 이상의 현역군인에 대한 작전통제권"을 가진 "전쟁-전투사령부"가 될 것이라고 주장합니다.[3]

연합사와 함께 "유엔사"의 임무는 한국 정전 유지, 비무장지대 통제, 판문점지역 경계, 주일 군사기지 유지, 그리고 미래 위기 발생 시 다시 한국으로의 외국군 진주계획을 세우는 것입니다. 특히 7개 주일 "유엔사-후방" 군사기지 사용을 존속시키고자 합니다.

앞서 지적했듯이 현재 일본의 "유엔사-후방" 사무실에는 오직 4명의 "유엔사" 대원만이 있습니다. 더구나 평택 캠프 험프리의 "유엔사령부"의 최근 군인 수는 웹사이트에 보이는 단체사진에 따르면 약 40명 정도로 나타납니다.

따라서 주한 "유엔사령부"와 주일 "유엔사-후방"사령부 해체는 현재 한국의 전반적인 군사 안정성에 거의 영향을 미치지 않을 것입니다. 게다가 그런 조치는 미국 정부가 한국 및 일본과 함께 양자의 상호방위조약 하에 그들이 주둔하고 있다고 주장하고 있기 때문에 한국과 일본의 미군의 존재에 어떠한 영향도 미치지 않을 것입니다.

3. 퇴물이 된 "유엔사" 재활성화 시도

지난 10년 동안 미국 정부는 끔찍한 "유엔사"를 되살리기 위해 작은 조치들을 취해 왔습니다. 2010년 호주는 "유엔사-후방"사령부를 지휘할 장교

---

3 www.usfk.mil/about/combined-forces-command

1명을 제공하기로 합의했습니다. 2011년 캐나다는 3명의 장교를 "유엔사" 사령부로, 1명을 "유엔사-후방"사령부로 파견했습니다. 2014년까지 미국 정부는 "유엔사령부" 참모를 확대하기 위한 보다 공식적인 다국적 인력배치"를 추진하기로 결정했습니다. 특히 "유엔사"는 작전(U-3) 및 병참(U-4), 2015년 이후엔 보강된 "U-3내 다국적조정센터(MNCC)"참모보좌관의 역할을 강화했습니다.**4**

이 재활성화프로그램의 주된 목적은 미래에 "전투목적을 위해" 사용될 수 있도록 "유엔사"의 능력과 준비태세를 높이는 데 있는 것 같습니다.**5** 이 프로그램의 또 다른 목적은 "유엔사"의 작전을 실제 국제 군사작전처럼 보이게 하는 것 같습니다.

이러한 노력은 2018년 1월에 미국 정부와 캐나다 정부가 캐나다에서 "한반도 안보 및 안정에 관한 밴쿠버외무장관회의"를 공동주최하면서 정치적 차원의 성질을 띠게 되었습니다. 이 회의는 트럼프 정부가 "유엔사" 회원국을 중심으로 대북제재를 위한 "최대 압박"실행을 주도하기 위한 것이었습니다. 이 회의에서 주목할 만한 한 명의 존재는 일본 외무장관이었습니다. 이것은 아마도 미국 정부가 미래에 일본을 "유엔사"의 공식회원국으로 합류하도록 할 것이라는 표시일 것입니다.

밴쿠버 회의가 있은 지 몇 달 후 미국 정부는 캐나다 중장(육군)을 "유엔사"의 첫 번째 비미국 부사령관에 지명함으로써 캐나다에 보답했습니다. 그런 다음 2019년 7월 미국 정부는 "유엔사" 차기 부사령관이 될 호주 제독(해군)을 임명했습니다. 또한 "유엔사"는 2020년에 마침내 자체 웹사이트**6**를 만들었습니다.

---

4 Creamer, pp.17-19

5 "S. Korea Peace Drive Complicated by 'Revitalization' of UN Command," *Financial Times*, Oct. 2, 2018

과거에 그들의 웹 사이트는 주한미군 웹사이트에 포함되어 있었습니다. "유엔사"는 전력파견국인 "호주, 벨기에, 캐나다, 콜롬비아, 덴마크, 프랑스, 그리스, 이탈리아, 네덜란드, 뉴질랜드, 노르웨이, 필리핀, 남아프리카공화국, 태국, 터키, 영국, 미국과 전력수여국인 대한민국"으로 구성됩니다. 이 목록은 "유엔사"의 회원국이 변경되었음을 보여줍니다.

처음 회원국은 "유엔사"와 한국에 전투병력을 제공한 16개국으로 구성되었습니다. 그러나 룩셈부르크와 에티오피아는 각각 1953년과 1965년에 "유엔사"에서 탈퇴했습니다. 그러나 노르웨이, 덴마크, 이탈리아는 각각 1999년, 2000년, 2013년에 "유엔사"에 가입했습니다. 이들 세 회원국이 한국에서 전투 재개 시 "유엔사"에 부상자를 위한 의료지원을 제공할지, 전투부대를 제공할지 여부는 분명하지 않습니다. 더욱이, "유엔사"의 옛 회원국들이 앞으로 다시 가짜 "유엔사"에 전투병력을 제공할 의지가 있는지 여부 또한 현재로서는 분명하지 않습니다.

밴쿠버 '유엔사' 참전국 외무장관회의

결국, 1950년에 안보리결의 83호와 84호에 제공된 원래의 권한과 임무가 이미 만료되었다는 강력한 주장이 제기될 수 있습니다. 즉, 향후 한국에서 새로운 전투가 발생하면 "유엔사"가 자체적으로 다시 전쟁을 벌일 법적 권한이 없다는 것입니다. 유엔안보리로부터 새로운 승인을 받아야합니다. 이같은 결론은 이 문제를 검토한 두 명의 법률전문가에 의해 뒷받침됩니다.

> "강력한 정책적 이해관계들은 안보리 스스로 명시적이고 명백하게 지속하지 않는 한 정전의 성립을 통해 안보리의 무력사용 권한을 종료하는 것이 현명하다."[7]

즉, 1953년 정전과 함께 1950년 안보리결의 83호와 84호는 종료되었다고 봄이 타당합니다.

4. 한국전쟁의 지속을 위한 "유엔사" 명칭 도용

과거 "유엔사"를 유지하기 위한 미국 정부의 주된 논리는 "유엔사"가 한국 정전협정의 당사국이므로 "정전협정 유지를 위한 대안적 합의"가 만들어지기 전에는 해체될 수 없다는 것이었습니다.[8] 그러나 이 논리에는 몇 가지 문제가 있습니다.

첫째, 미국은 "유엔사" 이름으로 서명한 정전협정에 대한 법적 권한을 가지고 있을까요? 안보리결의 84호가 미국 정부에 "유엔사" 명칭 사용을 승

---

[7] Jules Lobel and Michael Ratner, "Bypassing the Security Council: Ambiguous Authorizations to Use Force, Cease-Fires and the Iraqi Inspection Regime," *The American Journal of International Law*, Jan. 1999; Vol. 93, pp.144-145.

[8] A/RES/3390 (XXX) A, 1975

인한 바가 결코 없기에 그 답은 "아니오"입니다. 더구나 협정 자체가 법적 계약에 대한 기본적 요구조건을 충족하는데 실패했기 때문에 불법이자 무효입니다.

둘째, 미국이 정전협정 유지를 위한 상호합의를 진지하게 모색했다면 왜, 한국 정부에 남한군의 작전통제권을 돌려주듯이 그리고 또 한국군에게 "유엔사"의 일부 임무를 반환하듯이, 조선민주주의인민공화국에 상응한 제안을 하지 않을까요?

셋째, 누가 정전협정 유지에 대한 대안적 합의를 막고 있습니까? 조선민주주의인민공화국 정부는 1974년부터 미국 정부에 평화협정을 제안했고 1997년부터 1999년까지 4자회담(한·조·미·중)에 참가했습니다. 두 개의 한국은 유엔에 가입하고 "남북군사공동위원회" 설치를 포함, 역사적인 불가침 합의에 서명했습니다. 또한 양국 정상은 2018년 3차례 남북정상회담을 개최했고 2018년 9월 19일 포괄적인 군사분야합의서를 체결·비준했습니다. 가장 최근의 이 합의에도 남북군사공동위원회설치 서약이 포함됐습니다.

안타깝게도 이 남북군사합의는 미국 정부의 반대와 지속적인 통제로 인해 제대로 이행되지 못했습니다. 예를 들어 마이크 폼페이오 전 미 국무장관은 2018년 9월 남북군사합의서와 관련해 한국의 강경화 외무장관에게 "불만"을 표명했습니다.[9]

요컨대, 한국 지도자들은 미국 정부가 한국군에 대한 전시작전 통제를 계속 유지하는 한, 1953년의 낡고 산산조각 난 한국 정전협정을 대체하거나 평화협정에 서명하기 위한 어떤 대체 군사협정도 이행할 수 없습니다. 따

---

[9] *Reuters*, Oct. 18, 2018

라서 정전협정 유지를 목적으로 "유엔사"를 유지하고 있다는 미국 정부의 변명은 가짜입니다. 게다가 미국 주도 "유엔사"는 1958년 한국으로 핵무기를 반입하며 정전협정 무효를 선언한, 정전협정의 가장 심각한 위반자입니다.

사실 미국 정부는 한반도의 상시적 평화보다 현 정전체계를 유지하는 것을 좋아하는 것 같습니다. 미국 정부가 큰 희생의 한국전쟁을 끝내기 위한 평화협정 서명을 거부하는 데에는 몇 가지 무언의 이유가 있습니다.

1) "유엔사"의 이름으로 모든 남북교류와 경제활동을 포함, DMZ 지역에 대한 전반적인 통제 유지하기.
2) 남한에 더 비싼 무기를 팔려는 미국 군수회사들을 위해 한국의 전쟁상태 유지하기.
3) 한국에서 미군기지와 군대 유지하기입니다.

1983년 미합참 지시에 따라 "유엔사령관"은 한국에서 적대행위 재개 시 "유엔사 군대의 고용, 별개의 법적·군사기구로 유엔사와 연합사를 유지"하라는 임무를 부여받았습니다.[10]

"유엔사" 총사령관으로서 미군사령관이 연합사라는 이름 하에 한국군을 계속 통제하는 한 모든 외국 참전군과 한국군을 최종적으로 지휘·통제하게 될 것입니다.

---

10 "미합참의 유엔사령관을 위한 관련약정"1983.1.19.; "US CJCS Terms of Reference for Commander UNC," January 19, 1983

VI 결론

에이브러햄 링컨은 심오하고 감동적인 연설로 유명합니다. 그 중 하나는 거짓말에 관한 것입니다.

"당신은 모든 사람을 일시적으로 속일 수 있고, 일부 사람을 항상 속일 수 있지만, 모든 사람을 항상 속일 수는 없습니다."

우리가 한국전쟁 초기에 세워진 "유엔사"라는 웅장한 건물이 정교한 거짓말 위에 세워진 것을 밝히면서, 링컨의 지혜로운 말이 정말 진실로 들립니다. 이 팜플렛이 유엔기관으로서의 "유엔사"라는 오랜 신화에 약간의 빛이라도 비추어 주었길 바랍니다.

미국 정부가 죽어가는 "유엔사"를 되살리려고 하는 지금, 한국전쟁의 지속과 한국과 일본에 대한 지배를 위해 "유엔사"를 계속 활용하려는 냉전 전사들에게 더 이상 속지 않도록, 한국민과 국제사회가 "유엔사"의 진짜 정체와 그 거짓말을 이해하는 것이 더욱 중요합니다.

가짜 "유엔사"에 대한 우리 조사 결과와 분석을 요약하면 다음과 같습니다.

1) 유엔안전보장이사회는 1950년 7월 7일 "유엔사"를 설립하지 않았습니다. 안보리는 단지 유엔회원국이 미국의 "통합사령부"에 그들 병력을 제공하도록 "권고"만 했습니다.

2) 트루먼 행정부는 안보리결의 84의 채택 즉시 "통합사령부"를 창설했습니다. 그러나, 정치와 선전 목적으로 미국 정부는 1950년 7월 25일(한국 시간) 도쿄에 "유엔사령부"라는 새로운 군사사령부를 설립했습니다. 미국 정부는 때에 따라 어떤 목적에 맞추어 두개의 명칭중 하나를 사용했기 때문에 두 실체에 대해 많은 혼란이 있었습니다.

두 명칭은 한 동전의 양면과 같습니다. 1950년 유엔을 장악하고 있던 미국 정부는, 한국 내전에 대한 군사개입을 유엔의 "경찰조치"로 정당화하기 위해, 미국이 주도하는 외국군을 "유엔군"으로 묘사하기 위해, 미군 통제 하에 남한군을 예속시키기 위해, 그리고 한국전쟁에 일본의 협력을 유발하기 위해 유엔체계와 이름을 남용했습니다.

3) 문제의 안보리결의 82, 83, 84호는 유엔헌장의 많은 조항을 위반하여 적법한 절차없이 신속하게 채택되었습니다. 그것들은 대부분 불법이었습니다. 더욱이 미국 정부는 유엔결의가 취해지기 전조차 한국에서 일방적 조치를 취하거나, 유엔헌장이나 유엔결의의 언어나 단어의 의미를 왜곡함으로써 유엔헌장을 종종 훼손했습니다.

4) 비록 미국 장군이 1953년 한국 정전협정에 "유엔사"라는 이름으로 서명했지만 "유엔사"는 미국 정부의 이해관계만을 대변했기 때문에 유엔은 정전협정의 당사자가 아닙니다. 사실, "유엔사"는 출생의 시작부터 오직 미국 정부의 통제 하에 있었습니다. 휴전협정 자체의 합법성도 의심의 여지가 많습니다.

5) 통합사령부와 "유엔사"의 원래 임무는, 1953년에 휴전협정이 서명된 후 미군을 제외한 모든 외국군이 남한을 떠났을 때, 유엔총회가 1975년 "유엔사" 해체 결의를 채택했을 때, 남북한이 1991년 회원국으로서 유엔에 가입하고 불가침협정에 서명했을 때, 또는 2018년 평화를 위한 포괄적인 남북군사협정이 서명되었을 때 오래 전에 종료되었습니다.

6) 유엔 법무실은 1994년 "소위 '유엔사령부'가 잘못된 명칭임"을 확인하는 법적 의견을 발표했습니다.

7) 미국 주도 "유엔사"는 그 통제 하에 한국군을 예속하고, 영토를 점령하고, 남북한의 평화와 발전을 위한 협력을 방해함으로써 한국의 주권을 침해했습니다.

8) "유엔사"는 여전히 외국의 간섭 없이 한국 국민 스스로 한국의 영구적 평화, 진정한 독립, 통일을 이루는 데 큰 걸림돌이 되고 있습니다.

9) 유엔의 모든 회원국과 유엔 관리들은 유엔헌장을 유지하고 유엔 이름을 보호하기 위해 유엔의 보조기구도 유엔기관도 아닌 가짜 "유엔사"를 해체할 법적 책임이 있습니다.

10) 무엇보다도 미국 정부는 유엔헌장에 따라, 자신의 통제 하에 있는 가짜 "유엔사"와 빈사 상태의 통합사령부(미국 정부)를, 하루속히 해체할 가장 무거운 법적 책임이 있습니다.

특히 유엔헌장 제2조 2항은 "모든 회원국은 이 헌장에 따라 그들이 맡은 의무를 성실하게 이행해야한다"고 요구하고 있습니다. 유엔회원국의 기본 의무는 유엔헌장 제1조 및 제2조에 명시된 대로 유엔의 목적과 원칙에 따라 행동하는 것입니다. 다시 말해 미국 정부는 유엔의 이름을 남용하여 한국 주권을 침해하거나 한국민의 자결, 평화, 발전에 대한 기본적 인권을 계속 거부할 수 없습니다. 현 미국 행정부는 1975년 유엔총회 회의에서 미국무장관 헨리 키신저가 한 오래된 약속을 기억하길 바랍니다. "미국은 한국전쟁이 끝난 지 20년이 지난 지금, 유엔사령부를 종료하는 것이 시의적절하다는 데 동의한다."

자, 지금은 70년이 지났습니다.

더욱이 한. 일 양국 정부는 가짜 "유엔사"와의 협력 거부를 포함, 자신의 영토에서 떠날 것을 요구하고, 그에 대한 합법적 조치를 취하는 등 자신의 영토에서 가짜 "유엔사"를 해체하기 위해 필요한 모든 조치를 취할 중대한 책임이 있습니다.

마지막으로, 세계 시민사회를 포함한 세계인도 가짜 "유엔사" 해체를 위해 목소리를 높일 책임이 있습니다. 특히, 한.미.일 시민사회단체가 끝없고 값비싼 한국전쟁을 평화협정과 함께 최종적으로 종식시키기 위해 가짜 "유엔사"를 해체할 수 있도록 함께 일해야 하겠습니다.

만약 당신이 오랫동안 지연된 가짜 "유엔사"의 종료를 믿는 개인 또는 단체라면, 우리 웹사이트에 게시된 가짜 "유엔사령부" 해체를 위한 선언에 서명해주십시오. 2023년 한국 정전협정 70주년이 되는 시점까지 이러한 해체가 확실히 이루어지도록 합시다.

"유엔사령부"를 해체하라!
이제 끝없는 한국전쟁을 끝내자!

부록A

가짜 "유엔사령부" 해체를 위한 선언서

1950년 7월 7일, 유엔안보리는 결의84호(S/1588)를 채택하여 미국이 이끄는 '통합사령부' 설립을 회원국들에 권고했으나, 미국은 안보리 결의를 위반하고 "유엔사령부"를 설치했다.

1994년 부트로스 부트로스-갈리 유엔사무총장이 명확히 했고, 2018년 9월 로즈마리 디칼로 유엔사무차장이 안보리에서 재확인했듯이 소위 "유엔사"는 "유엔의 활동도 전문기구도 아니며 유엔의 지휘·통제 하에 있지도 않다."

더구나, 안보리 결의 84호 채택 자체가 소련의 "동의투표"가 없었기에 유엔헌장 위반이자, 유엔 상징과 깃발에 대한 총회결의와 1947년 12월 19일 첫 유엔깃발법의 위반이었다.

1975년 11월 18일, 유엔총회는 "'유엔사령부'를 해체할 필요가 있다'는 결의 3390B를 채택하여 유엔 이름의 남용을 막기 위한 담대한 조치를 취했다. 더욱이, 1953년 정전협정, 1970년 말 미국을 제외한 모든 외국군의 한국 철수, 1991년 남북한 유엔 동시 가입을 통해 안보리결의 84호의 목적이 이미 달성되었기에, 미국은 진즉에 "유엔사"를 해체했어야 했다.

그러나, 미국은 이 가짜 기구를 해체하는 대신, 한국에 수십억 달러의 미국 무기 수입을 강요하며, 북한에 대한 전쟁을 지속하기 위해서, 최근에는 죽어가던 "유엔사"를 부활시키려 하고 있다.

게다가, 2018년 미국은 비무장지대를 통과하는 철도·도로망 연결 같은 남북개발사업을 막기 위해서 남측 비무장지대의 관할권을 강변하고 "유엔사"의 임무를 확장했다.

이같은 퇴행적 움직임은 한반도에서 종국적인 평화와 화해, 협력, 발전을 위해 뛰고 있는 한국민의 강렬한 열망에 반하는 새로운 장애물이다.

따라서, 우리는 한국민의 평화와 정의에 대한 권리를 지지하는, 관심있는 개인과 단체로서, 가짜 "유엔사"의 신속한 해체를 촉구하는 이 선언서에 서명한다.

1. 소위 "유엔사"는 유엔의 전문기구도 보조기구도 아니다.

2. 미국은 가짜 "유엔사"의 유엔기 사용을 중단하라.

3. 미국 통제 하의 주한"유엔사"와 주일"유엔사-후방"을 즉시 해체함으로써 유엔 이름의 남용을 중단하라.

4. 미국은 "유엔사" 해체와 "한국정전협정을 평화협정으로" 교체할 것을 촉구한 1975년 유엔총회 결의를 이행하라.

5. 모든 유엔회원국과 시민단체들을 포함한 국제공동체는 유엔의 이름과 존엄을 수호하기 위하여 가짜 "유엔사"와의 모든 협력을 거부하고, 현혹된 실체의 종료를 앞당길 의무가 있다.

6. 가짜 "유엔사"의 조기 해체는 남북정상 합의의 이행과 한국전쟁의 공식적인 종결과 한국민의 완전한 자결권 행사와 국제적 차원의 유엔법과 국제법 발전에 기여할 것이다.

2021년 10월 12일
가짜 '유엔사' 해체를 위한 국제캠페인
(선언서를 지지하면 www.fakeunc.org에 방문하여 서명해 주십시오)

부록B —실행위원회

이장희	(사)평화통일시민연대 상임공동대표 (실행위원장)
류경완	(사)코리아국제평화포럼 공동대표 (사무총장)
권오혁	사무국장
이시우	사진가
죤 김	변호사 (미국)
고은광순	평화어머니회 상임대표
정연진	Action One Korea 한국 상임대표
이기묘	Action One Korea 한국 상임대표
리미일	(사)코리아국제평화포럼 이사
박영태	(사)코리아국제평화포럼 이사
김종귀	민주사회를위한변호사모임 미군문제연구위원장
신엘라	진보당 자주통일국장

부록C— 지지단체와 개인들

1. 국내단체 및 인사

〈학계〉
조영건 (경남대학교 명예교수)
이장희 (외국어대학교 명예교수)
임헌영 (민족문제연구소장)
이재봉 (원광대학교 교수)
이래경 (다른백년 이사장)
최용기 (국립창원대 명예교수)

〈전문가〉
이시우 (사진가) / Lee Si-woo (Photographer)

〈법률가 단체 및 변호사〉
민주사회를 위한 변호사모임 미군문제연구위원회
박진석 (변호사)
심재환 (변호사)
김종귀 (변호사)
허진선 (변호사)
권정호 (변호사)
남성욱 (변호사)
박삼성 (변호사)
오민애 (변호사)

〈사회단체〉
고은광순 (평화어머니회)
여인철, 한성, 안승문 (평화연방시민회의)
이기묘, 홍근진, 정연진 (AOK)
윤기진 (국민주권연대)
이양수 (민주노동자전국회의)
한찬욱 (사월혁명회 사무처장)
이윤 (사월혁명회 대외협력위원장)
박행덕 (전국농민회총연맹)
장남수 (전국민주화운동유가족협의회)
김옥임 (전국여성농민회총연합)
한미경 (전국여성연대)
이규재 (조국통일범민족연합남측본부)
곽호남 (진보대학생네트워크)
권낙기 (통일광장)
권오헌 (양심수후원회)
한충목 (한국진보연대)
김수남 (우리민족연방제통일추진회의)
김진수 (전국빈민연합)
류경완 (코리아국제평화포럼)
최영찬 (빈민해방실천연대)
조순덕 (민주화실천가족운동협의회)
김명환 (민주노총)
이장희, 홍성미, 심종숙, 이창호, 신수식
　　(평화통일시민연대)
김기준, 이천동 (대한민국 평화 재향 군인회)
지철 (주권방송 대표이사)
김봉준, 이대수 (유라시아 평화의 길)

<개인>

남기방 (대전세종건설지부)

윤임식

이진영

<정당>

이상규 (진보당)

김종훈 (전 국회의원)

권의석 (진보당 대전시당)

정수환 (진보당 광주시당)

2. 국제단체

<국제민주법률가협회>

진 마이어 미국 변호사 (국제민주법률가협회장)

베냐민 야스민 (알제리 변호사)

마리오 (아이티 변호사)

에드레 올릴리아 (필리핀 변호사,
　　필리핀 민중변호사 전국 노조 대표)

라샤리 (파키스탄 변호사)

무하마드 가니 (파키스탄 변호사)

니로퍼 (인도 변호사)

<아시아-태평양법률가협회>

사사모토 준 (일본 변호사,
　　아시아태평양법률가협회 사무총장)

하산 아브라르 (파키스탄 변호사,
　　아시아태평양법률가협회 부회장)

3. 국외단체 및 인사

캐나다

미셸 초서도브스키 (캐나다 오타와,
　　오타와대 경제학 명예교수, 세계화연구소 연구소장)

타마라 로린츠 (캐나다 온타리오, 평화를 위한
　　캐나다여성의 목소리 국가위원회)

평화철학센터 (밴쿠버)

방글라데시

대안정책 개발연구

일본

후지이 가쓰히코 (일본 나고야시, 전쟁반대 네트워크)

이시이 히로시 (일본 도쿄도, 회사원)

이소가이 지로 (일본 아이치현, 작가)

정종순 (일본 나고야시, 개호복지사)

사카이 겐지 (일본 나고야시, 전쟁반대 네트워크)

야마모토 미하기 (일본 나고야시, 단체직원)

오자와 다카시 (일본 도쿄도, 일한민중연대전국네트워크)

와타나베 겐주 (일본 도쿄도, 일한민중연대전국네트워크)

기타가와 히로가즈 (일본 사이타마현, '일한분석' 편집인)

가토 마사키 (일본 도쿄도, 일한민중연대전국네트워크)

일한민중연대전국네트워크

조선의 자주적 평화통일 지지 일본위원회

기무라 히데토 (일본 나가사키,
　　나가사키 재일 조선인의 인권을 지키는 모임)

박수경 (일본 나가사키)

후나카와 슌이치로 (일본 사가)

오가타 타카호 (일본 후쿠오카)

이토 칸지 (일본 후쿠오카)

소메키 토미요 (일본 나가사키)

카네사키 아키라 (일본 후쿠오카)
이시카와 아키코 (일본 후쿠오카)
하마구치 마리코 (일본 후쿠오카)
쿠와노 야수오 (일본 야마구치,
    시모노세키 일본과 한국을 잇는 모임)
아베 후쿠요시 (일본 후쿠오카)
미즈구치 요코 (일본 후쿠오카)
츠보이 히데오 (일본 오이타)
미즈구치 쓰네미쓰 (일본 후쿠오카)
가지와라 도구사부로 (일본 오이타)
산토 타다요시 (일본 후쿠오카)
카시와기 테류요시 (일본 후쿠오카)
수에나가 토시카즈 (일본 후쿠오카)
미구치 모토무 (일본 후쿠오카)
마츠자키 히로미 (일본 후쿠오카)
모투무라 마코토 (일본 후쿠오카)
수에나가 히로미 (일본 후쿠오카)
우라하타 카즈히사 (일본 오이타)
산마루 쇼코 (일본 오이타)
구로가와 도시에 (일본 후쿠오카)
나카가와 마사미 (일본 후쿠오카)
타데이시 도시오 (일본 후쿠오카)
시게토 에이치 (일본 후쿠오카)
하가 아키오 (일본 후쿠오카)
무라타 카즈코 (일본 후쿠오카)
와타나베 히로코 (일본 후쿠오카)
스즈키 마사아키 (일본 후쿠오카)
후루카와 나츠카즈 (일본 후쿠오카)
타시로 마사미 (일본 나가사키)
스가우치 타카오 (일본 후쿠오카)
오노 야스노리 (일본 후쿠오카)

호소이 아케미 (일본 도쿄도, 시민의 의견회)
한일 스톤워크 코리아
일본국제법률가협회

스웨덴

아그네타 노버그 (스웨덴 스톡홀름,
    스웨덴 평화협의회의장.
    우주 무기와 핵을 반대하는 글로벌 네트워크 이사)
스웨덴 평화이사회

미국

우주 무기와 핵을 반대하는 글로벌 네트워크
활동소나위협에 반대하는 시민들
오인동 (615 미국위원회 공동위원장)
미주 양심수후원회 / 김시환 / 회원 송영애 / 왕용운
민중당 뉴욕연대 / 한익수
조국통일범민족연합 재미본부
재미동포전국연합회 / 김현환
진보의 벗 / 하용진
전쟁 너머 세계 (본부, 미국 버지니아)
앨리스 슬레이터 (미국 뉴욕, 전쟁 너머 세계)
에이미 하리브 (미국 뉴욕,
    평화·정의 지구와의 조화를 위한 요가)
아리얼 키 (미국 캘리포니아, 평화 예지가)
밥 레이놀즈
부르스 개그넌 (미국 메인,
    우주 무기와 핵을 반대하는 글로벌 네트워크)
러셀 레이 (미국 메인, 활동소나위협에 반대하는 시민들)
나타샤 메이어즈 (미국 메인, 메인주시각예술가협회)
윌리엄 그리핀 (미국 펜실베니아, 평화보고서)
캐롤 어너 (미국 오레곤, 평화와 자유를 위한 국제 여성
    연맹)

챨스 류 (폴스 유나이티드 감리교회)
크라이스톰
데이비드 게인즈빌
크리스토퍼 헬리 (다트머스 대학교)
데니스 아펠 (미국 캘리포니아, 카톨릭 노동자)
데모인 카톨릭 노동자
다이아나 본 (미국 캘리포니아,
　　버클리시 평화 및 정의위원회 위원)
도날드 한
에르드만 팔모어
프랭크 코다로 (미국 아이오와, 카톨릭 워커스)
프랭크 스콧
전쟁반대 환경주의자들 (미국 캘리포니아)
자넷웨일 (미평화재향군인회)
캐슬린 윌리엄스
린발 드패스
래리 에글리
마크 크라이어
문장 (뉴욕 민중당)
존 캐시치
존 스타인마이어 (미평화재향군인회)
짐 골프포트
멜리사 플래밍
홀리 그라함 (미국, 수행자)
유지연 (한국정책연구원)
구한 백 만더 (미국 하와이)
린다 노벤스키 (미평화재향군인회)
전미한미협회
패스리샤 헤더리아
램지 림 (미국 메사추세츠, 보스턴대학 명예교수)
채닝, 포우파이 브루클린 교육재단
평화행동 (메인주)

평화노동자
포파이리엠 교육재단
한국장로교평화네트워크
수바라타 고시로이 교수 (미국 메사추세츠, 도쿄공대
　　과학기술사회연구제휴프로그램객원교수,
　　메사추세츠공대교수)
윤길상 목사
샐리 앨리스 톰슨
김수복 (6.15 미국위원회 위원장)
스티브 리빙스턴 (시카고 반전연합)
세인트 컬럼반 선교협회
평화재향군인회-한국평화캠페인
워싱턴화해모임
윌리엄 스위트

영국

엔지 젤터 (영국 슈롭셔, 2012년 노벨평화상 후보 및
　　트라이던트 플라우쉐어 설립자)
데이브 웹 (영국 웨스트요크셔, 국제 평화국 부소장,
　　우주 무기와 핵에 반대하는 글로벌 네트워크 의장,
　　핵무기 해체를 위한 영국 캠페인 위원장)
린디스 퍼시 (영국 노스요크셔,
　　미군기지 감시를 위한 캠페인 공동창립자)
트라이던트 플라우쉐어, 평화

인도

아루나 캄밀리아 (인도 비샤카파트남,
　　다모다람 산지바야 국법대학 조교수)
바부라오 카밀리아 (인도 비샤카파트남)
사이 하나쓰 아빌라시 둘리푸디 (인도 카르나카타)
뱅카타 아킬레시 둘리푸디 (인도 카르나카타)
잠무 나라야나 라오 (인도 우주 무기와 핵을 반대하는
　　글로벌 네트워크 이사)

호주

마릭빌 평화그룹 (호주 뉴사우스웨일스)

닉 딘 (호주 뉴사우스웨일스, 마릭빌평화그룹의장)

호주 반기지 운동 연합

데니스 도허티 (호주 시드니, AABCC 전국 코디네이터)

한나 미들턴 박사 (호주 시드니,
    AABCC의 우주전쟁반대활동가)

쉐린 히바드 (호주 쿡, 팔머스턴 럭키스쿨교장)

가번 막코맥 (호주 국가대학교 은퇴 교수,
    "냉전/온전" 저자)

독일

파울 쉬나이스 (독일 하이델베르그)

6.15유럽위원회

국제적 책임을 위한 과학자-기술자 국제네트워크

part 2

Real Identity of the "United Nations Command" (UNC) and Its Problems

Foreword

In year 2020, we observed the 70th anniversary of the outbreak of the Korean War-one of the longest wars that have never ended officially. Coinciding with this historic anniversary was also the 70th anniversary of the establishment of the so-called "United Nations Command"(UNC) in July 1950. Many books dealing with the Korean War have been written in the last 70 years. Unfortunately, almost all of these books provide scant attention on the real identity and role of the "UNC." Is this a UN entity? If not, who created it and why? What is the mission of this dubious entity, and why is it still present in Korea today?

Is it in South Korea to preserve peace or block the South-North reconciliation and exchanges? The answer was clear when it took negative steps in blocking the inter-Korean cooperation projects in 2018. Thus, in order to end the forever Korean War and achieve a peaceful reunification of Korea, we believe that it is imperative for the Korean people to work with the American and Japanese people to remove the presence of U.S.-led "UNC" from Korea and Japan as soon as possible. How can we do this?

We believe that the first step in realizing this goal is to educate ourselves as to the real history and identity of this strange, omnipotent "UNC," which is not under the direct control of the United Nations. It is very unfortunate, but it is likely that a large majority of people in South Korea today may still believe that the "UNC" is a military entity of the United Nations that was established by the UN in the early part of the Korean War. We will try to show in this pamphlet that this story is not true.

Other questions to be dealt in this pamphlet include when the "UNC" was established, the legal basis for the military entity, how its mission and role has changed over the years, its negative impact on Korea, Japan, U.S., and UN, etc. Our answers to these questions are based on historical documents of the UN, U.S., ROK, and Japan as well as various books, articles, and news reports.

Frankly, it was not easy to find the hidden history of the "UNC," but not impossible. In search for the truth, we found some shocking evidences that showed how the U.S. officials had tried to deceive the American people, the Korean people, and the world about their real role in the UN and the Korean War--all in the name of the UN. In this regard, the "UNC" myth certainly has played a major part in the American propaganda war that was launched from the beginning of the Korean War in 1950. The "UNC" is neither "a legitimate United Nations agency" nor an oldest "collective security enforcement army" of the UN. What the "UNC" has done in Korea in the past was neither a "police action" of the UN nor was it engaged in a "United Nations action" in Korea. Moreover, the foreign troops of the "UNC" did not represent "UN Forces." In fact, they were just a U.S.-led multinational force or coalition force.

It is about time for us to uncover all the misconceptions about the "UNC" and throw them away finally. That is the best way to free ourselves from the old myth and lies. This is especially important if the people in South Korea and Japan want to gain their full independence and national sovereignty from the shackles of the "UNC." In particular, the ROK Government's efforts to regain its wartime operational control from the U.S. military will be in vain, as long as the "UNC" is allowed to operate in South Korea. After all, the "UNC" is merely another military tool controlled by the US military and Washington officials.

When people of the world understand this truth accurately, the international community can make a strong demand to the USG to dissolve the "UNC," instead of reviving it. We hope that this pamphlet will help more people understand the real identity and dark history of the "UNC" so that they can join in the international call for the immediate dissolution of the fictitious "UNC." Such termination will not only serve the interest of the Korean, Japanese, and American people but also the purposes & principles of the United Nations by ending at last the long, illegal abuse of the UN Charter and its name in the last 70 years.

Professor. Emeritus Jang-Hie Lee
Chair of the Steering Committee
International Campaign to Abolish the Fake "UNC"

Seoul, September 8, 2021

I

"UNC" Is Not a Specialized Agency or Subsidiary Organ of the UN

The United States Government (USG) usually claims that the U.S.-led "United Nations Command" was established pursuant to the UN Security Council Resolution 82 (June 25, 1950), Resolution 83 (June 27, 1950), and Resolution 84 (July 7, 1950). In addition, the USG also claimed in the past that its troops were sent to Korea in 1950 for a "police action" of the UN to restore peace and security there, as part of the "UN Forces." These propaganda claims have misled many American and Korean peoples, as well as the international community, to believe that the so-called "United Nations Command" was established by the UN, as a Specialized Agency or Subsidiary Organ of the United Nations.

However, these claims and beliefs are quite misleading. For instance, the current website of "UNC" claims, "Following North Korean aggression against South Korea, United Nations Command (UNC) was established on July 24, 1950. It also talks about "the unified command we know as UN Command."[1] But it is silent as to who created the "UNC." What are the real facts and truth? In order to understand the real identity and problems of the "UNC," it is necessary to examine carefully how the initial Security Council Resolutions (SCR)—82, 83, and 84—were adopted soon after the outbreak of armed conflict in Korea on June 25, 1950 (Korean Time); whether they were adopted in accordance with the UN

---

1 *See* www.unc.mil, "About"

Charter; what the Resolutions stated; and whether the Resolutions were implemented faithfully or not.

1. Problems in the Security Council Resolution 82 of June 25

According to Article 24 of the Charter of the United Nations, the Security Council (SC) has "the primary responsibility for the maintenance of international peace and security." Chapter VII of the Charter provides the specific procedure and authority of the Security Council in dealing with situations where there exists any "threat to the peace, breach of the peace, or act of aggression" in the world.

Article 39, in particular, requires the Security Council 1) to "determine the existence" of the above-mentioned three acts first, and then 2) make "recommendations, or decide what measures shall be taken in accordance with Articles 41 and 42, to maintain or restore international peace and security."

In the afternoon of June 25, 1950 (ET, US), the SC held its first meeting, at the request of the U.S. Government, to discuss the outbreak of an armed conflict in Korea. In his message to the UN Secretary-General, the Deputy Representative of the U.S. Mission to the UN simply alleged that "North Korean forces invaded the territory of the Republic of Korea at several points in the early morning hours of June 25 (Korean Time)" according to a cablegram from the U.S. Ambassador in Seoul. The U.S. Representative then accused North Korea of committing "a breach of the peace and an act of the aggression."[2] The SC also considered a cablegram from the UN Commission on Korea in Seoul, which also made similar allegations: The "Government of South Korea states that

---

2   S/1495. The 'S' means the Security Council, and the '1495' means the serial number of official document.

about 4 am hrs 25 June attacks were launched in strength by North Korean forces all along the 38th parallel line." However, this cablegram also contained a different news report from North Korea:

> "Pyongyang Radio allegation at 13:35 hrs.(Korean Time) of South Korean invasion across parallel during night…also stated People's Army instructed repulse invading forces by decisive counter attack…"[3]

Thus, it is apparent that there was a dispute as to the origin of the armed conflict that happened on June 25. Under the circumstances, it was incumbent upon the SC to invite representatives of both Governments of Korea to the SC meeting to have a fair hearing on the dispute. Article 32 of the UN Charter states as follows:

> "….any state which is not a Member of the United Nations, if it is a party to a dispute under consideration by the Security Council, <u>shall be invited to participate</u>, without vote, in the discussion relating to the dispute."
> (Underline added)

Although the U.S. Mission brought in the South Korean Ambassador to the U.S. (John M. Chang) to the SC meeting on June 25, where he repeated again the allegations of the ROK Government and urged a speedy action by the UN, the SC decided not to invite a representative of the DPRK Government (North Korea) to attend the meeting.

In order to hear directly from the other party, the Representative of Yugoslavia (Mr. Bebler), a Member of the SC at the time, introduced a resolution, which called for "an immediate cessation of hostilities and withdrawal of troops" and invited "the Government of North Korea to state its case before the Security Council."[4] But this resolution was rejected by USG and its five allies, in the absence of the USSR and PRC (whose seat was still taken by a representative of Chiang Kai-Shek in Taiwan), with three

---

3 S/1496

Members (Egypt, India and Norway) abstaining from voting.

If the Yugoslavia's resolution was adopted, who knows whether the North Korean troops could have stopped their advance into the South? In a rush of judgment, the SC ended up adopting the U.S.-sponsored, one-sided Resolution 82,[5] determining that North Korea was responsible for

UNITED NATIONS

SECURITY COUNCIL

GENERAL
S/1501
25 June 1950
ORIGINAL: ENGLISH

RESOLUTION CONCERNING THE COMPLAINT OF AGGRESSION
UPON THE REPUBLIC OF KOREA ADOPTED AT THE 473RD
MEETING OF THE SECURITY COUNCIL ON 25 JUNE 1950

The Security Council

Recalling the finding of the General Assembly in its resolution of 21 October 1949 that the Government of the Republic of Korea is a lawfully established government "having effective control and jurisdiction over that part of Korea where the United Nations Temporary Commission on Korea was able to observe and consult and in which the great majority of the people of Korea reside; and that this Government is based on elections which were a valid expression of the free will of the electorate of that part of Korea and which were observed by the Temporary Commission; and that this is the only such Government in Korea";

Mindful of the concern expressed by the General Assembly in its resolutions of 12 December 1948 and 21 October 1949 of the consequences which might follow unless Member States refrained from acts derogatory to the results sought to be achieved by the United Nations in bringing about the complete independence and unity of Korea; and the concern expressed that the situation described by the United Nations Commission on Korea in its report menaces the safety and well being of the Republic of Korea and of the people of Korea and might lead to open military conflict there;

Noting with grave concern the armed attack upon the Republic of Korea by forces from North Korea,

Determines that this action constitutes a breach of the peace,

I. Calls for the immediate cessation of hostilities; and

Calls upon the authorities of North Korea to withdraw forthwith their armed forces to the thirty-eighth parallel;

/II. Requests
S/1501

> S/1501
> Page 2
>
> II. Requests the United Nations Commission on Korea
> (a) To communicate its fully considered recommendations on the situation with the least possible delay;
> (b) To observe the withdrawal of the North Korean forces to the thirty-eighth parallel; and
> (c) To keep the Security Council informed on the execution of this resolution;
>
> III. Calls upon all Members to render every assistance to the United Nations in the execution of this resolution and to refrain from giving assistance to the North Korean authorities.

Ref. 1, S-1501 RESOLUTION CONCERNING THE COMPLAINT OF AGGRESSION UPON THE REPUBLIC OF KOREA ADOPTED AT THE 473RD MEETING OF THE SECURITY COUNCIL ON 25 JUNE 1950

"a breach of peace," based on allegations from the South Korean officials only. (Ref.1) In doing so, the SC created much doubts on the fairness and legality of its action under the UN Charter. (Ref. 1, SCR[6] 82, S/1501, June 25, 1950)

Moreover, the Truman administration immediately abused SCR 82 by sending U.S. military weapons to the horrific regime of Syngman Rhee in the South and also ordering U.S. Air Force and Navy to attack North Korean forces. On June 27, 1950, President Truman stated as follows:

> "The Security Council called upon all members of the United Nations to render every assistance to the United Nations in the execution of this resolution (SCR 82). In these circumstances I have ordered United States air and sea forces to give the Korean government troops cover and support." (Parenthesis added)

This statement shows that the Truman administration interpreted "every assistance" in the Part III of SCR 82 in a far-fetched, overbroad way, as if the sentence in question authorized the use of force in defense of South

---

4 S/1500
5 S/1501
6 'SCR' is an abbreviation of Security Council Resolution.

Korea. This was nothing more than a blatant distortion of the Resolution 82, which mainly appealed for an "immediate cessation of hostilities" and the withdrawal of North Korean forces "to the 38th parallel." The call for "cessation of hostilities" applied to all sides, including both Governments of Korea as well as their military allies, including USG. By attacking North Korean troops on or about June 27-28(Korean Time), prior to any decision of the SC to use force in Korea, the Truman administration committed aggression against DPRK, in addition to violating SCR 82.

The Truman administration's a quick, unilateral military action against North Korea at this time cannot be underestimated in its impact: Such a move transformed what it had regarded as a domestic conflict in Korea into a dangerous international war involving major powers in the Far East. In taking the dangerous step, USG also severely violated the UN Charter to a large extent, including Articles 2(2), 2(3), 2(4), 2(5), and 2(7) of the UN Charter.

In particular, there are much doubts whether the SC had any jurisdiction to intervene in the Korean conflict in the first place since the UN Charter specifically prohibits UN's intervention in the internal affairs of a country. Article 2 (7) of the UN Charter states as follows:

> "Nothing contained in the present Charter shall authorize the United Nations to intervene in matters which are essentially within the domestic jurisdiction of any state; but this principle shall not prejudice the application of enforcement measures under Chapter VII." (Underline added)

When the two Korean states emerged in 1948, neither the Republic of Korea (ROK) in the South nor the Democratic People's Republic of Korea (DPRK) in the North recognized the other government. Each claimed to represent the whole Korea. This is not surprising--considering the long history of a united Korea for more than 1,000 years. It is also to be noted that the Truman administration itself regarded the ROK as the only lawful government in South Korea, and did not recognize DPRK as a legitimate, independent State. Thus, Truman explained the Korean situation in his press conference on June 29 as follows:

> "It (ROK) was unlawfully attacked by a bunch of bandits which are neighbors of North Korea (South Korea)...And the members of the United Nations are going to the relief of the Korean Republic to suppress a bandit raid on the Republic of Korea." (Underline and parenthesis added)

In other words, the Truman and his advisers took the position that the Korean armed conflict that erupted in June amounted to a domestic disturbance only. Taking a similar position, the text of SCR 82, which was drafted by the U.S. Department of State, also reflected Truman's view that the Korean conflict was an internal disturbance by calling the Korean People's Army of the DPRK as "forces from North Korea" and the Government of DPRK as "authorities of North Korea."

On the other hand, the SC took a different position on the nature of the Korean conflict by determining the existence of a "breach of the peace" in Korea when it adopted its Resolution 82. According to Prof. Hans Kelsen, a leading expert on the UN law, the SC's initial determination on the "breach of the peace" was a mistake:

> "Peace or, as the Charter says, 'international peace' is a relation between states. Hence a 'breach of the peace' can be committed only by a state in its relation to another state. If the 'forces from North Korea' are not the armed forces of a state and the 'North Korean authorities' not the government of a state but a revolutionary group or insurgents, and, consequently, the war in Korea a civil war, then the Council could not determine the existence of a breach of the peace; it could only determine a threat to the peace."[7] (Underline added)

Since there were no valid grounds for determining the existence of breach of the international peace or threat to the international peace in

---

7   Hans Kelsen, *The Law of the United Nations*, (New York: Frederick A. Praeger, 1951), p.930

the Korean situation at the time, the UN certainly had no legal authority to intervene in the domestic conflict of Korea in June 1950. The situation in Korea at the time did not qualify for the exception of "enforcement measures under Chapter VII" under Article 2(7) of the UN Charter.

Nevertheless, the Truman administration took the Korean issue to the United Nations because the U.S. officials were confident that the U.S. and its allies had the necessary votes to pass any resolutions they wanted from the SC-especially in view of the fact that the Soviet Union was boycotting the SC meetings at the time. In addition, it was also very useful for the USG to depict its war in Korea as a UN police action, for propaganda purpose, to the people in Korea, Japan, the U.S. and the rest of the world.

2. Problems in the Security Council Resolution 83 of June 27

On June 27, 1950, the SC held its second meeting on the Korean situation to review several cablegrams from the UN Commission on Korea, which suggested to SC to give consideration of either inviting "both parties agree on neutral mediator to negotiate peace or requesting Member Governments undertake immediate mediation."[8] The U.S. Representative ignored this suggestion and rushed to introduce another draft resolution, which recommended Members of the United Nations "furnish such assistance to the Republic of Korea as may be necessary to repel the armed attack and restore international peace and security in the area."(Underline added)

The only Article explicitly allowing direct UN enforcement action by use of force is Article 42 under Chapter VII, but due to the Cold War, the SC never assembled a UN Force of its own, even though this

---

8   S/1503, June 26, 1950

was envisioned in Article 43 of the Charter. In any case, the Truman administration was unwilling to use Article 42 in dealing with the Korean conflict for various reasons, including maintaining maximum freedom in its military action, lack of time to set up UN forces, etc. Thus, the USG ended up in using the "recommendations" language in Article 39, for the first time in the UN's history.

However, Prof. Kelsen thinks that the original framers of the UN Charter did not intend such recommendations to include any use of force. Thus, he states that, "under Article 39," the SC "cannot recommend enforcement measures; <u>it can recommend only peaceful means for the adjustment of a situation</u>," which is determined by SC to be a threat to, or breach of, the international peace.[9](Underline added) Therefore, SCR 83, which recommended the use of force to Members of UN implicitly, was illegal if the UN Charter is interpreted strictly in accordance with the original intention of the Charter framers.

The second problem with Resolution 83 is that any SC decisions on substantive matters require an affirmative vote of seven members at the time, "including the concurring votes of the permanent members" under Article 27(3). Thus, the USSR (Soviet Union) notified the UN on June 29 that SCR 83 was illegal since it was adopted "in the absence of two permanent members of the Security Council, the USSR and China"(People's Republic of China). Incidentally, the Soviet Union had been boycotting the SC meetings from mid-January 1950, in protest against the continuing seating in the SC of a representative of Chiang Kai-shek regime in Taiwan. The Soviet Union also complained that SCR 83 was illegal because it was adopted with only six yes votes, if not counting the vote of the representative of Chiang.[10]

---

9   Kelsen, p.932
10 S/1517

Unfortunately, no Member of the SC raised any questions about these legal issues at the time when draft SCR 83 was reviewed. Furthermore, no Member dared to criticize the Truman's public announcement about noon time on June 27 (ET, U.S.) that he had ordered the U.S. air and naval forces to bomb North Korean forces. This order was sent out long before SCR 83 was adopted, in violation of many provisions of the UN Charter, including Article 2(4). In consequence, the afternoon SC meeting of June 27 turned into a mere exercise of a rubber stamp, approving the unilateral use of force in Korea by the USG. Under a strong U.S. pressure, SCR 83 was eventually adopted on the same day, about 11 p.m., with one negative vote by Yugoslavia and two abstentions (Egypt and India). (Ref. 2) The Truman administration was so anxious to pass this Resolution quickly that it did not even allow enough time for the Governments of Egypt and India to consider the proposed draft and send any instructions to their representatives in New York. Also, the SC again allowed the ROK Representative to sit at the SC and make a strong appeal for military help, while no DPRK representative of was invited to speak at the meeting. (Ref. 2, SCR 83, S/1511, June 27, 1950)

At this critical time in the development of the Korean conflict, Truman's arrogance and hypocrisy was in full display: He was tearing apart the UN Charter as well as the U.S. Constitution violently, while he was claiming in his public announcement of June 27 that "the United States will continue to uphold the rule of law."[11]

3. Problems in the Security Council Resolution 84 of July 7

According to the autobiography of the first UN Secretary-General at the time, he claimed that it was he and his advisers who had prepared a new

---

11 "Text of President Truman's Announcement," *UPI*, June 27, 1950

and to refrain from giving assistance to the North Korean authorities.

Adopted at the 473rd meeting by 9 votes to none, with 1 abstention (Yugoslavia).[10]

83 (1950). Resolution of 27 June 1950

[S/1511]

The Security Council,

Having determined that the armed attack upon the Republic of Korea by forces from North Korea constitutes a breach of the peace,

Having called for an immediate cessation of hostilities,

Having called upon the authorities in North Korea to withdraw forthwith their armed forces to the 38th parallel,

Having noted from the report of the United Nations Commission on Korea[11] that the authorities in North Korea have neither ceased hostilities nor withdrawn their armed forces to the 38th parallel, and that urgent military measures are required to restore international peace and security,

Having noted the appeal from the Republic of Korea to the United Nations for immediate and effective steps to secure peace and security,

Recommends that the Members of the United Nations furnish such assistance to the Republic of Korea as may be necessary to repel the armed attack and to restore international peace and security in the area.

Adopted at the 474th meeting by 7 votes to 1 (Yugoslavia).[12]

84 (1950). Resolution of 7 July 1950

[S/1588]

The Security Council,

Having determined that the armed attack upon the Republic of Korea by forces from North Korea constitutes a breach of the peace,

Having recommended that Members of the United Nations furnish such assistance to the Republic of Korea as may be necessary to repel the armed attack and to restore international peace and security in the area,

---

[10] One member (Union of Soviet Socialist Republics) was absent.

[11] *Official Records of the Security Council, Fifth Year, No. 16*, 474th meeting, p. 2 (document S/1507).

[12] Two members (Egypt, India) did not participate in the voting; one member (Union of Soviet Socialist Republics) was absent.

Ref. 2, S-1511 SECURITY COUNCIL RESOLUTION 83 (1950) [ON ASSISTANCE TO THE REPUBLIC OF KOREA], 1950.6.27

SC draft resolution in order to create "some coordinating mechanism" for the UN efforts in Korea and "circulated it on July 3 to the United States, British, and French delegations, and to the President of the Security Council...Arne Sunde of Norway." His idea was to coordinate and supervise the various military forces of the Member States by establishing a SC "Committee on Coordination of Assistance for Korea," composed of seven UN Member States. His proposal also authorized the armed forces of a coalition of willing Members of the UN, acting under this resolution, to use the UN flag. Lie said that UK, France and Norway "liked the idea of such a committee," but the "United States Mission promptly turned thumbs down" on it because the "Pentagon was much opposed to such United Nations activity."[12] In any case, it is quite shocking to see that Lie made such a bold proposal since such steps would lead to a major violation of Chapter 7 of the UN Charter.

It is interesting to note that, on July 3, the U.S. Secretary of State Acheson also sent to the U.S. Mission to the UN a new draft resolution on Korea for the latter's comment. This draft contained the main features in the final SCR 84, except there was no paragraph on the use of the UN flag and the proposed committee of the SC had no real power.[13] It is not clear whether the U.S. Mission shared the U.S. draft with Lie or not. Considering his close relations with the USG, it is quite possible that Lie may have seen the U.S. draft and modified it as his own draft. In any case, it was quite unusual for the Secretary-General to circulate a draft SC resolution since he is merely an "administrative officer" of the UN. Anyway, the US Department of State revised its draft resolution on July 4 by incorporating some suggestions of Lie, such as the use of the UN flag. On July 6, a representative of the Norwegian Mission to UN asked the U.S. Mission whether the U.S. would agree to add the words "as agent for the United Nations" at the end of paragraph (3) of the draft resolution. But this proposal was rejected by the U.S. Mission.[14] In the end, the final draft deleted any reference to creating a coordination

---

12 Trygve Lie, *In the Cause of Peace*, (New York: Macmillan Co, 1954), pp.333-334
13 *Foreign Relations United States (FRUS)*, 1950, Korea, Vol. VII, Doc. 206
14 *FRUS*, 1950, Korea, Vol. VII, Doc. 229

committee within the SC. Thus, on July 7, the SC adopted its Resolution 84, which provided maximum freedom of action for the U.S. military with an aura of the UN blessing. (Ref. 3, SCR 84, S/1588, July 7, 1950)

For the sake of appearance, the Truman administration asked the U.K. and French Missions to the UN to co-sponsor the new SC resolution, and they agreed to do so. However, the USSR was still absent at the SC

**UNITED NATIONS
SECURITY
COUNCIL**

GENERAL
S/1588
7 July 1950
ORIGINAL: ENGLISH-FRENCH

RESOLUTION CONCERNING THE COMPLAINT OF AGGRESSION UPON THE REPUBLIC OF KOREA ADOPTED AT THE 476TH MEETING OF THE SECURITY COUNCIL ON 7 JULY 1950

The Security Council,

Having determined that the armed attack upon the Republic of Korea by forces from North Korea constitutes a breach of the peace,

Having recommended that Members of the United Nations furnish such assistance to the Republic of Korea as may be necessary to repel the armed attack and to restore international peace and security in the area,

1. Welcomes the prompt and vigorous support which governments and peoples of the United Nations have given to its Resolutions of 25 and 27 June 1950 to assist the Republic of Korea in defending itself against armed attack and thus to restore international peace and security in the area;

2. Notes that Members of the United Nations have transmitted to the United Nations offers of assistance for the Republic of Korea;

3. Recommends that all Members providing military forces and other assistance pursuant to the aforesaid Security Council resolutions make such forces and other assistance available to a unified command under the United States;

4. Requests the United States to designate the commander of such forces;

5. Authorizes the unified command at its discretion to use the United Nations flag in the course of operations against North Korean forces concurrently with the flags of the various nations participating;

6. Requests the United States to provide the Security Council with reports as appropriate on the course of action taken under the unified command.

Ref. 3, S-1588 RESOLUTION CONCERNING THE COMPLAINT OF AGGRESSION UPON THE REPUBLIC OF KOREA ADOPTED AT THE 478TH MEETING OF THE SECURITY COUNCIL ON 7 JULY 1950

meeting and three respected UN Member States (Egypt, India, and Yugoslavia) abstained from voting--showing their apparent disapproval of the Resolution. What were their concerns? It is likely that they had serious doubts about the legality of this Resolution under the UN Charter, including the use of the UN flag. Their abstention vote was fully justified since it turned out soon that the Truman administration started to abuse this Resolution to its liking.

Point 3 of the Resolution states that SC "recommends that all Members providing military forces... make such forces... available to a unified command under the United States of America" and Point 4 states that SC "requests the United States to designate the commander of such forces." (Underline added) In interpreting this Resolution, it is important to note that this document was not binding on all Members. It was up to each Member to decide whether to send any military forces or other assistance to Korea. In addition, it is also to be noted that SCR 84 did not use the expression of "United Nations Forces," in regard to the military forces to be sent to South Korea by Member States of the UN. Moreover, there was nothing said in this Resolution about the title of "UN Commander" or the name of "United Nations Command." If so, who created this kind of title and name?

On July 8, 1950, Truman announced that he designated Gen. Douglas MacArthur as "the Commanding General of the military forces which the members of the United Nations place under the unified command of the United States." Then, on July 10, the US Joint Chiefs of Staff(JCS) sent an official message to the Far East Command, informing MacArthur that he was designated by the President as "commander of the military forces assisting the Republic of Korea which are placed under the unified command of the United States." (Ref. 4, JCS Message, July 10, 1950, Truman Library)

Here again, there was nothing said of the "UNC" in the JCS message.

DEPARTMENT OF THE ARMY
STAFF MESSAGE CENTER
OUTGOING CLASSIFIED MESSAGE

~~SECRET~~
OPERATIONAL IMMEDIATE

PARAPHRASE NOT REQUIRED

Joint Chiefs of Staff
M M Stephens Capt US Navy
Executive Secretary JCS
55234

TO: CINCFE TOKYO JAPAN

INFO: CINCAL FT RICHARDSON ALASKA, CINCARIB QUARRY HEIGHTS CZ, CINCEUR HEIDELBERG GERMANY, COMGENUSFA (REAR) SALZBURG AUSTRIA, CINCPAC PEARL HARBOR TH, CINCIANT NORFOLK VA, CINCNELM LONDON ENGLAND, COMGENSAC OFFUTT AFB OMAHA NEBR, COMGENTRUST TRIESTE.

NR: JCS 85370   10 JUL 50

From JCS.

You have been designated by the President of the United States as commander of military forces assisting the Republic of Korea which are placed under the unified command of the United States by members of the United Nations in response to the resolution of 7 July of the Security Council of the United Nations. You are authorized to use at your discretion the United Nations flag concurrently with the flags of other nations participating in operations against North Korean forces. The United Nations flag will be used only in operations against North Korean forces and will therefore not be used in connection with your mission with respect to Formosa.

The terms of this directive authorizing the use of the United Nations flag at your discretion have been approved by the President of the United States and supersede the implications in his press release, Washington, 8 July. (Info note: Text of Security Council resolution of 7 July will be transmitted to you).

ORIGIN: JCS

DISTR: NAVAIDE, CSAF, CNO, CSA

CM OUT 85370   (Jul 50)   DTG: 101714Z   rkh

DECLASSIFIED
E.O. 12065, Sec. 3-402
DOD Directive 5100.30, June 18, 1979

By NLT-____ NARS, Date 11-5-__

COPY NO. M-2

THE MAKING OF AN EXACT COPY OF THIS MESSAGE IS FORBIDDEN

Ref. 4, JCS 메시지, 1950년 7월 10일, Truman Library

In response, however, MacArthur sent a personal message to Truman on July 11, thanking Truman for his appointment of him as the "United Nations Commander of the international forces to be employed in Korea." (Ref. 5, MacArthur's Message, July 11, 1950, Truman Library)

```
                        SIGNAL CENTER
                         EAST WING
                        The White House

                                        11 July 1950


      TO   :  THE PRESIDENT
      FROM :  General Douglas MacArthur

              PERSONAL FOR PRESIDENT HARRY S TRUMAN

              Dear Mr President:
                          I have just received the announcement of your
      appointment of me as the United Nations Commander of the international
      forces to be employed in Korea and can not fail to express to you
      personally my deepest thanks and appreciation for this new expression
      of your confidence. I recall so vividly and with such gratitude that
      this is the second time you have so signally honored me. Your personal
      choice five years ago as Supreme Commander for the Allied Powers in Japan
      placed me under an intimate obligation which would be difficult for me
      to ever repay and you have now added to my debt. I can only repeat the
      pledge of my complete personal loyalty to you as well as an absolute
      devotion to your monumental struggle for peace and good will throughout
      the world. I hope I will not fail you.
                                      Most respectfully and faithfully,
                                      (Signed)  Douglas MacArthur

      Recd 110255Z/too late for delivery/ Capt. Dudley
```

Ref. 5, MacArthur's Message, 1950년 7월 11일, Truman Library

In turn on the same day, Truman sent a personal message to MacArthur, expressing his appreciation for MacArthur's message relating to the General's appointment as the "United Nations Commander of the international forces in Korea." (Ref. 6, Truman's Message, July 11, 1950, Truman Library)

```
                MESSAGES BETWEEN THE PRESIDENT AND GENERAL MACARTHUR



                                SIGNAL CENTER
                                  EAST WING
                                The White House

                                                        11 July, 1950

            TO    :  General Douglas MacArthur
            FROM  :  The President
            NR    :  WH 497    Filed 112035Z


                    Dear General MacArthur:
                        I deeply appreciate the letter and the
            spirit of your message relating to your appoint-
            ment as the United Nations Commander of the
            international forces in Korea. Your words confirm
            me dash if any confirmation were needed dash in
            my full belief in the wisdom of your selection.
                        With my warm regards and all good wishes,
            I am
                                        Sincerely yours,

                                        Harry S. Truman
```

Ref. 6, Truman's Message, 1950년 7월 11일, Truman Library

Thus, it seems that it was MacArthur himself who started to use his title as the "United Nations Commander" and Truman just confirmed that title in his personal message to MacArthur. However, there is one close confidant of Truman who states otherwise. According to Senator Tom Connally, who was the Chairman of the Senate Foreign Relations Committee in 1950, Truman told him and other key members of the Congress at a White House briefing on Korea, June 30, 1950, that "MacArthur was...the <u>UN commander</u> as well as the United States commander in the fighting."[15](Underline added) If this is true, then it was, after all, Truman himself who started using the UN title first.

As for the name of the "United Nations Command" itself, it was officially established as a separate military command in Tokyo on July 25, 1950, in the name of Gen. Douglas MacArthur. (Ref. 7, S/1629, July 25, 1950, Korean Time)

However, the "UNC" did not have a separate staff or facilities: Almost all the staff of the "UNC" was selected from the U.S. military officers who were working at the time as staff officers of the U.S. Far East Command in Tokyo.

The use of "UNC" name was nothing more than a deliberate abuse of the UN name. Whether MacArthur was using the name on his own initiative or under an order from Washington is not clear. As mentioned before, the JCS message of July 10 or Truman's announcement of July 8 did not direct MacArthur specifically to establish the "UNC" in Tokyo. However, there is one U.S. military history book which confirms that MacArthur acted under Truman's order: "On 10 July at the request of the United Nations, President <u>Truman directed</u> General MacArthur <u>to establish the United Nations Command</u>(UNC)..."[16](Underline added) It is

---

15 Tom Connally, *My Name is Tom Connally*, (Thomas Y. Crowell Company, 1954), p.349
16 Joint History Office, Office of the Chairman of the Joint Chiefs of Staff, *The History of the Unified Command Plan*, 1946-1999, 2003, p.19

UNITED NATIONS		
SECURITY		GENERAL
COUNCIL		S/1629
		25 July 1950
		ORIGINAL: ENGLISH

NOTE DATED 25 JULY 1950 FROM THE REPRESENTATIVE OF THE UNITED STATES OF AMERICA TO THE SECRETARY-GENERAL TRANSMITTING THE TEXT OF COMMUNIQUE NUMBER 135 OF THE FAR EAST COMMAND

The Representative of the United States to the United Nations presents his compliments to the Secretary-General of the United Nations and has the honour to request that there be brought to the attention of the Security Council the following Far East Command Communiqué Number 135:

(Released Tokyo 0850 Korean Time 25 July (EDT 1850 24 July))

The United Nations Command, with General Headquarters in Tokyo, was officially established today with General Douglas MacArthur as Commander-in-Chief
The announcement was made in General Order No. 1, General Headquarters, United Nations Command. The order reads:

"1. In response to the resolution of the Security Council of the United Nations of July 7, 1950, the President of the United States has designated the undersigned Commander-in-Chief of the Military Forces assisting the Republic of Korea. Pursuant thereto, there is established this date the United Nations Command, with General Headquarters in Tokyo, Japan.

"2. The undersigned assumes command.

"Douglas MacArthur
General of the Army,
United States Army
Commander-in-Chief"

Ref. 7, S_1629-UNC창설보고1950.7.25

possible that this book's history was based on a classified document containing the Truman's order in question, but such document, if there is one, is still not available to the public. In this regard, it is interesting to note how Truman himself saw the relationship between the "Unified Command" and "UN Command." In his memoirs, he stated as follows: "We were in Korea in the name and on behalf of the United Nations. The 'unified command' which I had entrusted to Douglas MacArthur was a

United Nations command."**17** (Underline added) In other words, he is saying that the two names are like the front and backside of a coin, and that he approved the name of the "United Nations Command" at least.

Nevertheless, there is another twist to this story. Ambassador Austin, the Permanent Representative of the U.S. to the UN HQ in 1950, explained at the SC meeting on July 31, 1950 that the "UNC" was merely a "field agency" of the UC (USG). That was a shocking statement, but an indirect admission by a high-level U.S. official that the "UNC" name had been created by the U.S. to suit its purpose. Such name was obviously intended to depict the U.S. military intervention in Korea as a UN mission and its troops as "UN Forces." In fact, the First Report of the UC (USG) to the SC described the multinational forces fighting in Korea as the "United Nations Forces" as well as "Unified Command forces."**18** Perhaps, other possible reasons for using the "UNC" name was to make it easier for other Member States to send their armed forces to Korea in the name of the UN, and also making it easier for the ROK forces to come under the U.S. operational control.

Point 5 of the Resolution states that the SC "authorizes the unified command at its discretion to use the United Nations flag in the course of operations against North Korean forces…." Indeed, this paragraph is the most troublesome part of the Resolution 84. The main question here is whether the SC had the power in 1950 to authorize the use of the UN flag to a Unified Command of multinational forces that would be engaged in military operations in Korea. The answer is no for two main reasons.

Under Chapter V or VII of the UN Charter, there is no specific authorization for the SC to regulate the use of the UN flag. In fact, by

---

17 Harry S. Truman, *Memoirs by Harry S. Truman*, Vol. 2, (William S. Konecky Associates, 1956), p.378
18 S/1626, July 25, 1950, ET

adopting Point 5 in the SCR 84, the SC violated the General Assembly (GA) resolution 167 (II) of October 1947, which had adopted the UN flag and authorized the Secretary-General, the chief administrative officer of the UN, "to adopt a flag code, having in mind the desirability of a regulated use of the flag and the protection of its dignity." In accordance with the GA resolution, then Secretary-General Trygve Lie issued the first UN Flag Code in December 1947. However, this Code contained no provision for the use of the U.N. flag in military operations. It was only on July 28, 1950, about 20 days after Resolution 84 was adopted, when the Secretary-General added a new paragraph to the UN Flag Code so that the flag could be "used in military operations only upon express authorization to that effect by a competent organ of the United Nations."(Section 6 of the Code) Nevertheless, Prof. Kelsen criticized the new paragraph as "ex post facto" justification of the Point 5 and reminded that "the only organ of the United Nations competent to authorize the use of flag was the Secretary-General" on July 7.[19] Thus, then Secretary-General Lie's attempt to assign his power to other UN organs was null and void since it violated the GA Resolution 167(II). Lie's efforts to authorize the use of UN flag for the UC, a non-UN entity, and his later amendment of the UN Flag Code to justify the SC's action of July 7 were quite reprehensible since his actions only undermined the interest and dignity of the United Nations.

In regard to the continuing use of the UN flag, there is also a legal question whether the "UNC" in Korea and the "UNC-Rear" in Japan can still use the UN flag at this time, when there are no military operations against North Korean forces. The language in Point 5 specifies that the UC may use the UN flag "in the course of operations against North Korean forces" only. This paragraph should be interpreted narrowly

---

[19] Kelsen, p.938

since it was added to Point 5 by the Representatives of U.K. and France as part of their efforts to limit the use of the UN flag.[20] This means that "UNC" and "UNC-Rear" should have stopped using the UN flag when the active fighting in Korea was halted with the Military Armistice Agreement in 1953.

Therefore, in September 2019, 46 concerned South Korean and other civil society groups in the world joined in the letter of International Association of Democratic Lawyers(IADL) to the UN Secretary-General Guterres, asking his opinion on the continuing use of the UN flag by the "UNC" in Korea and Japan. (Ref. 8, IADL Letter to the UN Secretary-General, September 30, 2019)

However, the Assistant Secretary-General for Legal Affairs of the UN responded in October 2019 with a short letter that "the questions you have asked concern matters that do not fall within the competence of the Secretary-General." (Ref. 9, Response from the UN Secretariat, October 10, 2019)

Unfortunately, the evasive letter failed to explain the legal basis of its conclusion and ignored the fact that the authority to authorize the use of the UN flag was delegated to the Secretary-General by the GA Resolutions 92 (I), 7 December 1946, and 167 (II), 20 October 1947.

UN flag flying over Camp White Beach in Okinawa

---

20 See *FRUS*, Doc. 229

IADL

CHAUSSÉE DE HAECHT 55, 1210, BRUXELLES-BRUSSELS, BELGIQUE-BELGIUM
info@iadllaw.org www.iadllaw.org

September 30, 2019

Hon. Antonio Guterres
Secretary-General
The United Nations
New York, New York
Sgcentral@un.org

Re: Seeking the Position of the UN Secretary-General on the Use of the UN Flag by the "United Nations Command" in Korea and Japan

Dear Secretary-General Guterres:

The International Association of Democratic Lawyers, (IADL) a non-governmental organization with consultative status with ECOSOC, is writing on behalf of itself and other civil society groups that are supporting this letter (the list of these groups is at p. 3). We are seeking your opinion on the above issue because the UN General Assembly adopted a resolution beginning in its early history to protect the name of the United Nations and Secretary-General had been authorized by the General Assembly to adopt a UN flag code and protect its dignity.[1]

1. The U.S. military is still using the UN flag at certain military bases in Korea and Japan, in claiming to be the "United Nations Command," which was unilaterally created by the U.S. in July 1950. The U.S. uses Security Council Resolution 84 of 7 July 1950 to justify its use of the UN flag. However, there are some serious problems with such use. For instance, the Security Council made a grave mistake in authorizing the use of the UN flag for a non-UN, multi-national military command that was only recommended in SCR 84. Perhaps, some members of the Security Council at the time may have believed that the Security Council had such power. However, according to Prof. Hans Kelsen, the leading legal scholar on the Charter and Law of the United Nations at the time, such opinion had "no basis neither in the Charter nor in the Resolution 167(II) of the General Assembly."[2] Moreover, SCR 84 authorized the "Unified Command" to use the UN flag in the "course of operations against North Korean forces," but the U.S. military has used the UN flag in the name of the "UN Command" in its military operations in Korea from the beginning.

2. The first UN Flag Code was issued on 19 December 1947, and Pt. 8 of the Code stated that "the flag shall not be used except in accordance with this Flag Code." However, the Code did not contain a provision authorizing the use of the flag in military operations. On 28 July, 1950, Secretary-General Trygve Lie added to the Code a new paragraph under Pt. 6 which stipulated that "the flag may be used in military operations only upon express authorization to that effect by a

---

[1] A/RES/92 (I), Official Seal and Emblem of the UN, 7 December, 1946; A/RES/167 (II), United Nations Flag, 20 October 1947.
[2] Hans Kelsen, *The Law of the United Nations: A Critical Analysis of Its Fundamental Problems* (New York: Frederick A. Praeger, 1950), p. 938.

1

Ref. 8, IADL Letter to the UN Secretary-General, September 30, 2019

However, as if accepting some of our points raised in our 2019 letter, the Secretary General revised the UN flag code on November 20, 2020, for the first time in 53 years since 1967. As a result, the "UNC" is now facing a strong challenge to its continued use of the UN flag in Korea and Japan, from the UN itself. We regard the revised UN flag code as the

United Nations  Nations Unies

HEADQUARTERS · SIEGE   NEW YORK, NY 10017
TEL.: 1 (212) 963.1234 · FAX: 1 (212) 963.4879

10 October 2019

Dear Ms. Mirer,

I refer to your letter dated 30 September 2019, addressed to the Secretary-General and sent on behalf of the International Association of Democratic Lawyers and certain other civil society groups, regarding the use of the United Nations flag by the United Nations Command in the Republic of Korea and Japan. You seek answers from the Secretary-General to certain questions of a legal nature on that subject.

I regret to have to inform you that the questions that you have asked concern matters that do not fall within the competence of the Secretary-General.

Yours sincerely,

Stephen Mathias
Assistant Secretary-General for Legal Affairs

Ms. Jeanne Mirer
President
International Association of Democratic Lawyers
Brussels

Ref. 9, Response from Mr. Mathias-UNC

---

first achievement of our movement and welcome it positively. (Ref. 10, ST/SGB/2020/4, new UN Flag Code 2020.11.20.)

Although not well known to the public, it turns out that the Office of Legal Affairs of the UN, in fact, reviewed the relationship between the Unified Command, the "United Nations Command," and the United

United Nations  **Secretariat**

ST/SGB/2020/4

20 November 2020

Secretary-General's bulletin

United Nations Flag Code

The Secretary-General, for the purpose of updating the provisions related to the protocol and use of the flag of the United Nations, hereby promulgates the following:

1. By resolution 167 (II), the General Assembly resolved that the flag of the United Nations shall be the official emblem as adopted in its resolution 92 (I), centred on a light blue background. By the same resolution, the General Assembly directed the Secretary-General to draw up regulations concerning the dimensions and proportions of the flag and authorized the Secretary-General to adopt a flag code, having in mind the desirability of the regulated use of the flag and the protection of its dignity.

2. Pursuant to that resolution, the Flag Code was first issued by the Secretary-General on 19 December 1947 and the Flag Consolidated Regulations on 23 July 1949.

3. The Code and Regulations were amended on 11 November 1952. The Regulations were further revised on 1 January 1967 and the Code and Regulations were promulgated as Secretary-General's bulletin ST/SGB/132.

4. The revised Flag Code, which consolidates the previously separate Flag Code and Flag Regulations into a single document, regulates the use of the flag and is annexed to the present bulletin.

5. The present bulletin shall take effect on the date of its issuance.

6. The Secretary-General's bulletin of 1 January 1967 entitled "The United Nations Flag Code and Regulations" (ST/SGB/132) is hereby abolished.

(*Signed*) António **Guterres**
Secretary-General

20-16047 (E)   031220

Please recycle

Ref. 10, ST/SGB/2020/4 개정된 유엔기법 2020.11.20.

Nations, and clarified this legal issue in a legal memorandum in 1994. The key conclusions in this legal memo were as follows: 1) "the Security Council did not establish the Unified Command as a subsidiary organ under its control;" 2) "The Unified Command in the Republic of Korea is similar to the allied military coalition set up in the Gulf war," and 3) "The so-called 'United Nations Command' is a misnomer."[21] The first point in the legal memo's conclusion was also reaffirmed by then UN Secretary-General Boutrous Boutrous-Ghali in his letter to the DPRK Foreign Minister on June 24, 1994. More recently, the distinction between the UN and "UNC"/UC was again clarified by a high-level official of the UN: Rosemary Dicarlo, the Under-Secretary-General for Political Affairs, who had also served as the former Deputy Representative of the U.S. Mission to the UN HQ for three years. In her briefing to the SC in 2018, on the relationship between the "UNC" and UN, she explained as follows:

"Notwithstanding its name, the United Nations Command is not a United Nations operation or body, nor does it come under the command and control of the United Nations. Furthermore, it was not established as a subsidiary organ of the Security Council and is not funded through the United Nations budget. As such, there are no reporting lines between the United Nations Command and the United Nations Secretariat."[22] (Underline added)

---

21 *UN Juridical Yearbook*, 1994, Chapter VI, pp.501-502
22 S/PV. 8353, September 17, 2018. PV means verbatim records of meeting.

"UNC" Has Violated Sovereignty of Korea

1. Subjugation of South Korean Military under U.S. Control

On July 25, 1950, the U.S. Mission submitted a letter to the UN Secretary-General, in which it was alleged that President Rhee of the ROK had sent a letter to General MacArthur on July 15, 1950, stating as follows: "I am happy to assign to you command authority over all land, sea, and air forces of the Republic of Korea during the period of the continuation of the present state of hostilities."(Underline added) MacArthur, in turn, sent a message to Ambassador Muccio (the U.S. Ambassador in South Korea) on July 18, asking the Ambassador to convey his "thanks and deepest appreciation for the action taken" by President Rhee.[1]

However, historians never found the original or a copy of the signed letter of Rhee. Moreover, the two messages were exchanged through U.S. Ambassador Muccio, who was closely following and guiding Rhee on all policy matters at the time-creating doubts about possible role of Muccio in drafting these messages. In particular, there are some difference in the date and content of Rhee's letter, when it is compared to Muccio's letter to Rhee, in regard to the same subject matter. For instance, Muccio sent a letter to Rhee on July 16 in which he stated that MacArthur had sent a message to Rhee, in response Rhee's letter of "July 14." In his letter, the

---

[1] S/1627, July 25, 1950

Ambassador stated that Rhee "designated to him (MacArthur) operational command authority over the land, sea and air forces of the Republic of Korea..."(Underline and parenthesis added). "Designated" is clearly different from "assigned" as shown in the Rhee letter sent to the UN. In addition, MacArthur's message is dated July 18 in the SC document, while Muccio's letter is dated July 16. It seems the document submitted to the UN contained more broad language than the one Muccio alleged. Thus, it is not clear as to the real content of President Rhee's letter and how and when the messages were exchanged.

In any case, Rhee's alleged assignment of his "command authority" was illegal under the ROK Constitution since this important matter was never discussed with his cabinet members and there is no record of any approval of it by his cabinet members. In addition, there was no co-signature to the important military document by Rhee's Prime Minister and Minister of Defense, as required by Article 66 of the Constitution. Furthermore, the U.S. and "UNC" violated the specific term in the SCRs 83, which only recommended that "Members of the United Nations furnish such assistance to the Republic of Korea...."(Underline added). Instead of providing necessary assistance to the ROK Government, the USG and the "UNC," in fact, took a full control of the ROK Government to a large extent - the command authority over the ROK military in particular - during the 1950-1953 period of the Korean War.

The assignment of "command authority" of the ROK military to Gen. MacArthur also raises other serious questions. Was the letter written by Rhee voluntarily or written by the U.S. Embassy? The U.S. officials were certainly in a position to dictate their wishes to Rhee at the time since his regime's survival was completely dependent on the help provided by the U.S. military. In fact, there were many instances in which the U.S. Ambassador, his staff, Gen. MacArthur, or his troops tried to control the movement and decisions of President Rhee or take over the authority of the various ROK Government agencies unilaterally, including the Ministry of Transportation and Ministry of Communications. By controlling Rhee, the U.S. Embassy became the real boss in South Korea at the time—even replacing the Chief of Staff of the ROK Army, Chae Byong-dok, and Rhee's Home Minister, Baek Song-uk.

According to Frank Baldwin, editor of the *Embassy at War*, a memoire of Harold J. Noble, who had served as First Secretary of the U.S. Embassy in South Korea as well as the political liaison officer to President Rhee, the Embassy "wanted the President out of the way during the summer of 1950 to prevent any political interference with the war effort." Thus, Ambassador John Muccio tried to keep Rhee away from his generals and cabinet members by asking him to move down to the South from one city to another—even though North Korean troops were far away from him. For instance, Rhee had to go down to Pusan and Taegu, staying there during the summer. It would not be an exaggeration to say that Muccio assumed the role of an acting President of South Korea from June to September 1950 in particular; and "President Rhee accepted a subordinate status temporarily and grudgingly."[2]

Above stories about the unequal, dubious relationships between President Rhee and the U.S. Embassy/Military in South Korea in the summer of 1950 indicate that the alleged exchange of letters between Rhee and MacArthur in regard to the alleged transfer of operational control of the ROK troops General MacArthur is highly unreliable. According to General Bradley, what actually happened to the South Korean troops at the time was that "Walton Walker (Commanding General of the 8th Army, U.S.) assumed tactical command of all UN forces in Korea,

---

[2] Harold Joyce Noble, Edited by Frank Baldwin, *Embassy at War*, (Seattle: University of Washington Press, 1975), p.xvi

including the ROK's, on July 13."³(Underline added) Thus, it is likely that there was no signed letter from Rhee to MacArthur. Perhaps, there could have been just a conversation between Rhee and Gen. Walker, or between Rhee and Ambassador Muccio.

The more shocking story in this subject matter is that the U.S-led "UNC" prepared a secret contingency plan called "Operation Ever-ready" to remove Syngman Rhee, who was called "a doddering old fool" by Harold J. Noble's private letter. According to declassified documents, the original plan was drafted in July 1952 by Gen. Mark W. Clark, the Commander of "UNC" and the Far East Command (U.S.) under the direction of the Joint Chiefs of Staff. At the time, the U.S. officials were worried whether Rhee's "repressive policies might provoke civil unrest and undermine the war effort." The plan-involving arrest of Rhee and setting up a "UNC" military government if necessary--was not carried out because Rhee, under pressure from the U.S., released detained opposition political leaders. The "UNC" also gave another serious consideration to the plan in May 1953 when Rhee threatened to oppose the Armistice Agreement being negotiated and pull out the ROK forces from the "UNC." To mollify Rhee, President Eisenhower had to agree to sign a security treaty with ROK, while asking Rhee to keep the ROK troops under the "UNC" control.[4]

Unfortunately, USG is still delaying or refusing to give up its wartime operational control over the ROK armed forces even today. This 70 year-long military control over the ROK military by the USG constitutes, indeed, a gross violation of the sovereign rights of the Korean people to determine their own military affairs.

---

3   Omar N. Bradley and Clay Blair, *A General's Life*, (Touchstone, 1983), p.543
4   "Papers Show U.S. Considered Ousting Rhee in Korean War," *The NYT*, August 4, 1975

2. Invasion and Occupation of North Korea

After a successful landing of some 70,000 troops at Inchon on September 15, 1950, the U.S.-led "UNC" continued to move on to retake Seoul, and then move toward the 38th parallel which divided the North and South. On September 27, the Joint Chiefs of Staff authorized MacArthur to cross the dividing line with a new military objective: "the destruction of the North Korean armed forces."[5] On October 1, the ROK Army I Corps "crossed the parallel and moved toward Wonsan."[6]

On the same day, from Tokyo, Gen. MacArthur issued his demand to the "North Korean Forces" to surrender. This message was transmitted to the UN by the U.S. Representative to the UN, New York, as a "Special Report of the Unified Command of the United Nations Forces in Korea." It is quite interesting to note that this Report described MacArthur's title as the "Commanding General of the Unified Command" and "United Nations Commander in Chief." In addition, the Unified Command was specifically referred to the "United Nations Forces in Korea," and

Photo taken after crossing the 38th parallel

5   Callum A. MacDonald, *Korea: the War Before Vietnam*, (New York: Free Press, 1986), p.49
6   Wada Haruki, *The Korean War: An International History*, (Lanham, MD: Rowman and Littlefield, 2014), p.126

the name of "United Nations Command" was also mentioned in the message.[7] This document provides clear evidence that the USG regarded the UC and "UNC" as the same entity.

In any case, by invading North Korea, the Truman administration violated the terms of the two SC resolutions dealing with the Korean situation. Under SCRs 83 and 84, Member States of the UN were only allowed to use force in Korea to "...furnish such assistance to the Republic of Korea as may be necessary to repel the armed attack and to restore international peace and security in the area."(Underline added) Considering the initial calls in the SC resolution 82—"cessation of hostilities" and the withdrawal of the North Korean forces "to the 38th parallel," it is clear that the intended meaning of "repel the armed attack" was to push back the North Korean troops to the 38th parallel and then possibly achieve a cease-fire agreement. American officials also confirmed this objective initially in private and public. On June 29, Acheson declared that the U.S.military was fighting "solely for the purpose of restoring the Republic of Korea to its status prior to the invasion."[8]

However, the idea of invading and occupying North Korean territory began to circulate within the Truman administration from mid-July. On July 13, Gen. MacArthur told two Pentagon generals visiting him in Tokyo that he intended "to destroy...the North Korean forces. I may need to occupy all of North Korea."[9] MacArthur's view clearly reflected his desire to support the strong ambition of the militant, anti-communist crusader, Syngman Rhee, who had been preaching unification of Korea by marching to the North. Truman also asked his National Security Council (NSC) for a study on the same issue on July 17, and thus a report, "United

---

7 S/1829, 1 Oct. 1950
8 Joseph C. Goulden, *Korea: The Untold Story of the War*, (McGraw-Hill Companies, 1983), p.237
9 Goulden, p.234

States Courses of Action with Respect to Korea,"[10] was submitted to him. On September 11, Truman approved the Report, which suggested a new U.S. objective in Korea: "If the present UN action in Korea can accomplish this political objective (establishment of a united government under the ROK) without substantially increasing the risk of general war with the Soviet Union or Communist China, it would be in our interest to advocate the pressing of the UN action to this conclusion."[11] (Parenthesis added) The Report also recommended that the Joint Chiefs of Staff be authorized to "direct the Commander of the UN forces in Korea to make plans for the possible occupation of North Korea."[12]

A particular interest in this Report is a frank admission that "military actions north of the 38th parallel which go beyond the accomplishment of this mission (pushing back the North Korean forces to the 38th parallel)" to achieve other objectives, such as "<u>unifying Korea under the ROK, are not clearly authorized by existing Security Council resolutions.</u>" (Parenthesis and underline added)

Accordingly, the Report concluded that it was necessary to get a new "UN approval for military actions in furtherance of this political objective."[13] However, USG was apparently afraid of a possible veto by the Soviet Union in the SC because the Soviet Representative had already returned to the SC meeting on August 1, 1950. Thus, the Truman administration decided to take the matter to the General Assembly, and worked with the U.K. Mission to draft a resolution that would somehow approve the new objective of the UC that had been already decided in Washington to occupy the North Korean territory and establish a united

---

10 NSC-81/1, September 9, 1950
11 NSC-81/1, p.1
12 NSC-81/1, p.4
13 NSC-81/1, p.3, Paragraph 12

"Government of Korea." For the sake of appearance, the U.S. again asked the U.K. and other allies to co-sponsor the resolution.

After rejecting again an invitation to a representative of the DPRK Government to attend the General Assembly Meeting, the U.S.-dominated GA easily adopted a pro-U.S. joint resolution, under the title of "The Problem of the Independence of Korea," on October 7, 1950, with a voting result of 47 (yes)-5(no)-7(abstention). (Ref. 11)

The Resolution's title was quite misleading since nothing was mentioned about crossing the 38th parallel and occupying North Korea by military means. Nevertheless, the issue was somehow addressed indirectly, in vague terms with much flexibility for different interpretations, by *recommending* that "All appropriate steps be taken to ensure conditions of stability throughout Korea" (1a); the "establishment of a unified, independent and democratic government in the sovereign State of Korea" by holding elections "under the auspices of the United Nations" (1b); and the "United Nations forces" should remain "in any part of Korea" only until "achieving the objectives specified....above" (1d). In addition, the Resolution also created two subsidiary entities of the GA: 1) The "United Nations Commission for the Unification and Rehabilitation of Korea (UNCURK)" to represent the UN "in bringing about the establishment of a unified....government of all Korea;" and 2) an "Interim Committee (of UNCURK)...to consult with and advise the United Nations Unified Command" immediately, until the "arrival in Korea" of the UNCURK. (Parenthesis added) (Ref. 11, A/RES/376(5)[14], October 7, 1950)

Although the Truman administration skillfully obtained a fig leaf for its invasion and occupation of North Korea through the October 7 GA resolution, it cannot be denied such Resolution was adopted in a gross

---

[14] A/RES/376(5). 'A' means the UN General Assembly. 'A/RES/' means the Resolution of UN General Assembly.

VII

RESOLUTIONS ADOPTED ON THE REPORTS OF THE FIRST COMMITTEE

376 (V). The problem of the independence of Korea

The General Assembly,

Having regard to its resolutions of 14 November 1947 (112 (II)), of 12 December 1948 (195 (III)) and of 21 October 1949 (293 (IV)),

Having received and considered the report[1] of the United Nations Commission on Korea,

Mindful of the fact that the objectives set forth in the resolutions referred to above have not been fully accomplished and, in particular, that the unification of Korea has not yet been achieved, and that an attempt has been made by an armed attack from North Korea to extinguish by force the Government of the Republic of Korea,

Recalling the General Assembly declaration of 12 December 1948 that there has been established a lawful government (the Government of the Republic of Korea) having effective control and jurisdiction over that part of Korea where the United Nations Temporary Commission on Korea was able to observe and consult and in which the great majority of the people of Korea reside; that this government is based on elections which were a valid expression of the free will of the electorate of that part of Korea and which were observed by the Temporary Commission; and that this is the only such government in Korea,

Having in mind that United Nations armed forces are at present operating in Korea in accordance with the recommendations[2] of the Security Council of 27 June 1950, subsequent to its resolution[3] of 25 June 1950, that Members of the United Nations furnish such assistance to the Republic of Korea as may be necessary to repel the armed attack and to restore international peace and security in the area,

Recalling that the essential objective of the resolutions of the General Assembly referred to above was the establishment of a unified, independent and democratic Government of Korea,

1. *Recommends* that

(*a*) All appropriate steps be taken to ensure conditions of stability throughout Korea;

(*b*) All constituent acts be taken, including the holding of elections, under the auspices of the United Nations, for the establishment of a unified, independent

and democratic government in the sovereign State of Korea;

(*c*) All sections and representative bodies of the population of Korea, South and North, be invited to co-operate with the organs of the United Nations in the restoration of peace, in the holding of elections and in the establishment of a unified government;

(*d*) United Nations forces should not remain in any part of Korea otherwise than so far as necessary for achieving the objectives specified in sub-paragraphs (*a*) and (*b*) above;

(*e*) All necessary measures be taken to accomplish the economic rehabilitation of Korea;

2. *Resolves* that

(*a*) A Commission consisting of Australia, Chile, Netherlands, Pakistan, Philippines, Thailand and Turkey, to be known as the United Nations Commission for the Unification and Rehabilitation of Korea, be established to (i) assume the functions hitherto exercised by the present United Nations Commission on Korea; (ii) represent the United Nations in bringing about the establishment of a unified, independent and democratic government of all Korea; (iii) exercise such responsibilities in connexion with relief and rehabilitation in Korea as may be determined by the General Assembly after receiving the recommendations of the Economic and Social Council. The United Nations Commission for the Unification and Rehabilitation of Korea should proceed to Korea and begin to carry out its functions as soon as possible;

(*b*) Pending the arrival in Korea of the United Nations Commission for the Unification and Rehabilitation of Korea, the governments of the States represented on the Commission should form an Interim Committee composed of representatives meeting at the seat of the United Nations to consult with and advise the United Nations Unified Command in the light of the above recommendations; the Interim Committee should begin to function immediately upon the approval of the present resolution by the General Assembly;

(*c*) The Commission shall render a report to the next regular session of the General Assembly and to any prior special session which might be called to consider the subject-matter of the present resolution, and shall render such interim reports as it may deem appropriate to the Secretary-General for transmission to Members;

The General Assembly furthermore,

Mindful of the fact that at the end of the present hostilities the task of rehabilitating the Korean economy will be of great magnitude,

---

[1] See *Official Records of the General Assembly, Fifth Session, Supplement No. 16.*
[2] See *Official Records of the Security Council, Fifth Year,* No. 16.
[3] *Ibid.,* No. 15.

9

Ref. 11, A-Res-376(5) THE PROBLEM OF THE INDEPENDENCE OF KOREA, 1950.10.7 1951.1.1

---

violation of the Korean people's right to "self-determination" (Article 1(2)) of their political future on their own, including the peaceful reunification of the divided nation. The U.S. cannot abuse the UN system to impose a pro-U.S. or pro-ROK government on the North Korean people by use of force. Such a dubious resolution, while not binding on Member States of the UN, undermined greatly the UN Charter by its blatant violations of

Article 12(1), 11(2), Article 24, and Article 25, among others.

In particular, Article 12(1) prohibits the General Assembly from making "any recommendation" on certain dispute or situation, while the SC "is exercising in respect of any dispute or situation the functions assigned to it." Since the SC had been dealing with the armed conflict in Korea from June 25, 1950, the GA violated Article 12(1) when it adopted the Oct. 7 Resolution, recommending measures like 1a ("steps be taken to ensure conditions of stability throughout Korea"), 1d ("United Nations forces" may stay "in any part of Korea" until "a unified, independent and democratic government" is established in Korea) or 2b ("form an Interim Committee...to consult with and advise the United Nations Unified Command"). Due to a high risk of expanding the Korean conflict with China and Russia, from the crossing of the 38th parallel by the "UNC"troops, any approval of such a dangerous military move by the UN had to be approved first by the SC, which "has primary responsibility for the maintenance of international peace and security." In fact, the Korean issue remained on the agenda of the SC until it was removed officially by adoption of a resolution on January 31, 1951.[15]

In regard to the role of the Interim Committee (IC), its real purpose was revealed in its adoption of a resolution on October 12: The key part is in paragraph 4, "*Advises* the Unified Command to assume provisionally all responsibilities for the government and civil administration of those parts of Korea....which may now come under occupation of UN forces," pending further consideration by UNCURK.[16] (Underline added) In other words, the IC authorized the "UNC" forces to set up a military government in North Korea. Since the SC had been exercising its jurisdiction to deal with the armed conflict in Korea at the time, this IC resolution was also null and void. In short, it was illegal for the GA to recommend the foreign

---

[15] S/1995
[16] A/1881, p.13

troops of the "UNC" to commit aggression against the DPRK, occupy the North Korean territory, and establish a military government there.

Based on the illegal IC Resolution, the "UNC" tried to establish a UN military government in the North Korean towns and cities during October and November 1950, when it occupied most of the North Korean territory. At the same time, the Rhee regime's military, police, and anticommunist youth groups were setting up their own occupation administration in the same areas. Sometimes, "American Counter-Intelligence Corps teams, working with Korean police and youth groups, rounded up individuals found on KWP(Korean Workers' Party) membership lists," and many atrocities were committed against them.[17]

After the Armistice Agreement was signed in July 1953, the "UNC" ruled over about 13,000 Koreans who had resided in the former territory of North Korea--in certain areas below the DMZ but north of the 38th parallel--by setting up its military government in such areas, using the South Korean military units. After receiving persistent demands to turn over these areas, the "UNC" finally agreed to a "transfer of administrative control" only of these areas to the ROK Government, starting from November 17, 1954.[18] By retaining its military control over these areas between 38th parallel and Military Demarcation Line of South, the "UNC" has violated the sovereignty of the ROK Government.

Ceremony of transfer administrative control to the "restoration area" north of the 38th parallel. 1954.11.17

---

17 Bruce Cumings, *The Korean War: A History*, (Modern Library, 2010), pp.196-197
18 Monica Hahn, "A Study on the UNC's Occupation Policy and the Transfer of Administrative Control to the ROK in North Korea, 1950-1954," *Critical Review of History* (in Korean), Nov. 2008, pp.3

3. Obstruction of South-North Cooperation Projects

In recent years, the "UNC" in South Korea illegally assumed a new role as a regulator of approving or blocking South-North cooperation projects for peace and development. For instance, in August 2018, the "UNC" Commander refused to give a permission for a South Korean railroad car to travel to North Korea to conduct a joint survey of the railroad conditions in the North. The excuse for the denial was that the documents submitted by the South Korean Government were "insufficient." At the same time, the news report also indicated that the U.S. also interfered with the opening of an inter-Korean liaison office that South Korea wanted to open at Kaesong in North Korea by "complaining that bringing equipment and materials across the border could violate UN sanctions."[19]

Another more offensive incident happened on September 25, 2018, at the U.S. Senate Armed Services Committee hearing on the nomination of Gen. Robert Abrams as the next Commander of the "UNC," ROK-U.S. CFC, and USFK. When asked about the South-North summit held in Pyongyang, Gen. Abrams, who had served as the Commander of the "UNC" in Korea until July 2, 2021, commented about the South-North agreement of September 19, 2018 as follows: "While they may continue to (engage in) dialogue, all of that will have to be brokered, adjudicated, observed, and enforced by the UN Command."(Parenthesis added) In other words, the Korean officials may sign any economic or military agreement, but it will have to be reviewed and approved by the "UNC." Does that mean the Korean people have no sovereign rights over any South-North cooperation matters?

---

[19] "USFK Chief Blocks Survey of North Korean Railway," *The Chosunilbo*, August 31, 2018

In fact, the truth is that it is not the U.S. Generals who are deciding the U.S. policy in Korea. It is usually the Washington officials who make the final decision whether to approve or disapprove any South-North agreements. However, such U.S. interferences in the internal affairs of the Korean people, through the use of "UNC," violate the main purposes of the UN Charter in Article 2 ("to develop friendly relations among nations based on respect for the principle of equal rights and self-determination of peoples...") and Article 3 ("promoting and encouraging respect for human rights and for fundamental freedoms for all..."). The Korean people, whether they live in the South or North, are also entitled to enjoy fundamental human rights and freedoms for development, peace, travel, association, etc. No foreign government or international organization can deny such basic human rights and freedoms to the Korean people who have lived together as a united nation for more than 1,000 years.

Moreover, such interference in the inter-Korean relations by the "UNC" would constitute a violation of the original mission of the SCRs 83 and 84. These Resolutions had nothing to do with the subsequent non-proliferation sanctions of the UN against DPRK.

"UNC" Was Created in Violation of U.S. Laws

1. Violation of the "UN Participation Act"

After the U.S. ratified the UN Charter as an international treaty, becoming the first Founding Member of the United Nations on August 8, 1945, the U.S. Congress soon took steps to pass an implementation law which authorized and regulated the actual participation of the United States in the UN system. This new law, known as the United Nations Participation Act(UNPA), became effective on December 20, 1945. Section 6 of the UNPA[1] specifically dealt with the procedure of providing U.S. armed forces to the UN Security Council on its call. Article 43 of the UN Charter imposed an obligation on all Members of the UN, upon the call of the SC, to conclude "a special agreement" with the SC, in regard to "the numbers and types of forces…and assistance" to be provided.

Accordingly, the pertinent part in the Section 6 of the UNPA stated as follows:

> "The President is authorized to negotiate a special agreement or agreements with the Security Council which shall be subject to the approval of the Congress by appropriate Act or joint resolution, providing

---

1   22 U.S.Code §287d

for the numbers and types of armed forces, their degree of readiness and general location, and the nature of facilities and assistance, including rights of passage, to be made available to the Security Council on its call for the purpose of maintaining international peace and security in accordance with Article 43 of said Charter…"[2] (Underline added)

Section 6 of the UNPA clearly shows that it was also the understanding of the U.S. Congress that any U.S. participation in military actions of the UN to be undertaken required first "special agreements" between the SC and willing Member States of the UN. And such an agreement for the U.S. required the approval of both the House and Senate. However, President Truman and his advisers apparently decided to ignore these legal requirements. As pointed out earlier, the Pentagon was unwilling to subordinate the U.S. military forces under the command of the SC. In addition, the administration's officials wanted to avoid any questions or hearings on their decisions by the Congress. For instance, Secretary of State Acheson "did not want to risk exposing the decisions" of the administration "to possible attacks by legislators…, or to precipitate a general discussion of the ultimate costs or consequences of military intervention in the Korean fighting."[3]

Thus, the Department of State and Pentagon officials drafted the SC Resolution 83 in such a way to avoid the SC's control over any UN military action in Korea, and without the need to negotiate a special agreement with the SC. This meant for the Truman administration to ignore the requirements of Articles 42 and 43 of the UN Charter. In doing so, the administration's officials also failed to comply with the requirements of the UNPA, in particular the specific procedures provided for the participation of U.S. troops in military enforcement measures of the UN.

---

2 22 U.S.C. §287d
3 Glenn D. Paige, *The Korean Decision, June 24-30, 1950*, (Free Press, 1968), p.187

Nevertheless, hiding their real intentions, Truman and his advisers tried to justify their military actions in Korea in the name of the United Nations or as a "police action" of the UN. For instances, at the first Blair House meeting of high-level officials on the evening of June 25, 1950 (US, ET), General Bradley (Chairman of the Joint Chiefs of Staff) advised the participants that "we should act <u>under the guise of aid</u> to the United Nations," and President Truman stressed that "we are <u>working entirely</u> for the United Nations."[4] (Underline added) In addition, at a news conference on June 29, 1950, Truman tried to minimize the extent of the U.S. military intervention in Korea by describing his actions as a "police action" under the UN. That was a big lie since Truman already had approved a major military action against the Korean People's Army of DPRK by ordering U.S. Air Force and Navy to "give all-out support" to the South Korean forces, at the second Blair House meeting on the night of June 26.[5]

2. Violation of the U.S. Constitution

While the President serves as the "Commander in Chief" of the U.S. armed forces, the actual power "to declare War" belongs to the Congress under Article I, Section 8, clause 11 of the U.S. Constitution. In the past history, the President sometimes used U.S. war ships or troops to engage in minor combats abroad to save American lives or protect U.S. interests, without a formal declaration of war or authorization from the Congress. But in a major war, the President is required to obtain a formal declaration of war from the Congress, in accordance with Section 8 of Article I--either prior to the commencement of war or soon after the

---

4 *FRUS*, 1950, Korea, Volume VII, Doc. 86
5 Dean Acheson, *Present at the Creation*, (W.W. Norton, 1969), p.407

war started. There were five wars in which the U.S. Congress adopted a formal declaration of war: War of 1812, Mexican-American War, Spanish-American War, WW I, and WW II.

Although the U.S. courts were divided whether the Korean conflict was a war or not, the highest military court of the United States did not hesitate to issue a clear, strong opinion in the case of the Korean situation. In *United States v. Bancroft*, 3 C.M.A. 3, 11 C.M.R. 3, 3 U.S.C.M.A. 3, (1953),[6] the United States Court of Military Appeals stated as follows:

"A reading of the daily newspaper accounts of the conflict in Korea; an appreciation of the size of the forces involved; a recognition of the efforts, both military and civilian, being expended to maintain the military operations in that area; and knowledge of other well-publicized wartime activities convinces us beyond any reasonable doubt that we are in a highly developed state of war."[7] (Underline added)

Even if counting the U.S. troop casualties and cost of war only, the Korean War, in fact, ranks top fifth among all the U.S. wars. The U.S. casualties alone in Korea amounted to some 130,000 killed and wounded; and the U.S. cost of war--just counting for the 1950-1953 period--was about $390 billion, in 2019 dollars.[8]

Since the Korean War was a major war for the U.S., President Truman had a legal obligation, under the U.S. Constitution, to ask the Congress to adopt a declaration of war against the DPRK (North Korea) and PRC (China). He was required to take this step in particular, since his administration was not acting in accordance with Article 42 and 43 of

---

6 *United States v. Bancroft*, 3 C.M.A. 3, 11 C.M.R. 3, 3 U.S.C.M.A. 3, (1953) July 3, 1953 · US Court of Military Appeals · No.1139
7 Opinion by Judge George W. Latimer; two other judges concur
8 "U.S. Military Casualties of War," *Wikipedia*, accessed June 7, 2021 "Most Expensive Wars in U.S. History," 24/7 *Wallst*, June 7, 2019

the UN Charter and Section 6 of the UNPA. Moreover, even if assuming that the SCR 83 was legally valid, its recommendation was not binding upon the USG. It was up to each Member State of the UN to decide whether to intervene in the Korean civil war or not. The decision to wage war against the DPRK clearly belonged to the U.S. Congress--not to the President. However, Truman just gave two short briefings, at the White House on June 27 and 30, 1950, to the key leaders of the U.S. Congress about his decisions already taken to use the U.S. military forces in Korea but he never asked for an official declaration of war from the Congress. This constituted a clear violation of the U.S. Constitution.

In reaction to the unilateral actions of Truman, most members of the Congress remained silent due to the fear of McCarthyism. Nevertheless, there were a few brave members who criticized Truman's actions openly in the Congress. Among them were Senator Robert A. Taft (Rep-Ohio), Senator Kenneth S. Wherry (Rep-Nebraska), and Representative Vito Marcantonio (American Labor Party-NY). Senator Taft "warned that if the President could intervene in Korea 'without Congressional approval, he can go to war in Malaya or Indonesia or Iran or South America.'"[9] In the House of Representatives, Rep. Marcantonio declared as follows: "When we agreed to the United Nations Charter, we never agreed to supplant our Constitution with the United Nations Charter. The power to declare and make war is vested in the representatives of the people, in the Congress of the United States."[10] The Rep.'s statement is correct that a U.S. treaty cannot replace the U.S. Constitution, which is the highest law of the land.[11]

---

[9] Louis Fisher, "The Korean War: On What Legal Basis Did Truman Act?," *The American Journal of International Law*, Vol. 89:21, 1995, p.35

[10] *Ibid.*

[11] See Reid v. Covert, 354 U.S. 1, 17 (1956)

Unfortunately, as Senator Taft had warned so prophetically, Truman's unilateral war in Korea had a devastating impact in undermining the Congressional power over war in subsequent years, since his bad precedent was followed later by other U.S. Presidents such as Johnson in Vietnam, Cambodia, and Laos; Clinton in Yugoslavia; and Obama in Libya.

IV   "UNC" Has Violated Japan's Peace Constitution

1. Violation of Article 9's Prohibition Against "War Potential"

The post-WW II Constitution of Japan was first enacted by the National Diet on November 3, 1946 and became effective on May 3, 1947. It became famous in the world because it has an Article renouncing war as a national policy. Article 9 of this Constitution states as follows:

> "Aspiring sincerely to an international peace based on justice and order, the Japanese people forever renounce war as a sovereign right of the nation and the threat or use of force as means of settling international disputes. 2, In order to accomplish the aim of the preceding paragraph, <u>land, sea, and air forces, as well as other war potential, will never be maintained.</u> The right of belligerency of the state will not be recognized."[1]
> (Underline added)

Although there is still some misconception in the U.S. and Japan that General MacArthur was responsible for drafting the Article 9, it is now confirmed that the real credit for the Article belongs to Mr. Shidehara Kijuro, a former Foreign Minister of Japan, who was accepted as the first postwar Prime Minister of Japan in October 1945 by the U.S. military occupation authorities.[2] Instead of defending Article 9, McArthur

---

[1] https://japan.kantei.go.jp/constitution_and_government_of_japan/constitution_e.html
[2] James E. Auer, "Article Nine of Japan's Constitution," *Law and Contemporary Problems*, Spring 1990, pp.173-174

played a major role in undermining Article 9's legal prohibition against maintenance of any "war potential" or participation in war, during the early period of the Korean War in particular. For instance, on July 8, 1950, he "ordered the Japanese Government to establish a 75,000-man National Police Reserve and increase the Maritime Safety Force by 8,000 men."[3] The Yoshida Administration had to comply with this unconstitutional order because Japan was still under the U.S. military occupation at the time.

On July 13, 1950, at his Tokyo Headquarters, MacArthur told a visiting delegation of the U.S. Joint Chiefs of Staff that the "Japanese Police Force should be converted into a constabulary of four divisions, with American equipment to provide security for Japan."[4] Thereafter, the Japanese National Police Reserve was renamed as the "National Safety Forces" in October 1952, and it was again renamed as the "Self-Defense Forces" in July 1954. Thus, MacArthur, as Commander-in-Chief of the Far East Command (U.S.), Supreme Commander for the Allied Powers (SCAP) in Japan, and Commander-in-Chief, the "UNC," helped pave the way for Japan to rearm again, in violation of Article 9's prohibition against any standing military forces.

Today, Japan is recognized as one of the leading military powers in the world. Its annual military spending in 2020 was $49 billion-ranking 9th in the world. In comparison, South Korea spent $46 billion on its military in 2020.[5] Japan's Air Force power ranks 6th in the world with 1,480 warplanes; its Navy has 155 warships; and its Army has about 250,000 soldiers with about 1,000 tanks.[6] This kind of military strength

---

3   Wada, p.93

4   J. Lawton Collins, *War in Peacetime: The History and Lessons of Korea*, (Boston: Houghton Mifflin Company, 1969), p.83

5   *See* SIPRI Military Expenditure, 2020

6   www.globalfirepower.com

certainly constitutes a "war potential," and thus violates Article 9 of Japan's Constitution.

2. Japan's Participation in the Korean War

Japan's Constitution is putting a major emphasis on Article 9 by including it under a prominent, separate "Chapter II" with the title of "RENUNCIATION OF WAR". The first paragraph of Article 9 states that the Japanese people "forever renounce war as a sovereign right of the nation."Along with this paragraph, it is also helpful to read the Preamble of the Constitution to understand the reasons why Article 9 was included in the postwar Constitution of Japan. The first paragraph of the Preamble shows a strong determination of the Japanese people to avoid another horrible war like the Pacific War in WW II: "Never again shall we be visited with the horrors of war through the action of government." The second commitment in the Preamble is the Japanese people's desire for "peace for all time." The last point explains how Japanese people shall achieve their peace and security: by recognizing other people's "right to live in peace, free from fear and want," by trusting in "the justice and faith of the peace-loving peoples of the world," and by pursuing "peaceful cooperation with all nations…" Thus, in order to preserve Article 9, it is essential for Japan to avoid any military alliances with other military powers, refuse to allow its land to be used as military bases for other countries, and maintain friendly relations with all nations.

Unfortunately, to make Japan a military ally of the United States, the Truman administration has "pressured Japan to amend Article 9 and to rearm as early as 1948."[7] In particular, MacArthur, also known as

---

[7] Umeda, Sayuri, "Japan: Interpretations of Article 9 of the Constitution" (2015), www.loc.gov. Retrieved June 16, 2021

the "American Caesar," played a major role in turning Japan into a major participant in the Korean War, in violation of Article 9. First of all, MacArthur set up the military Headquarters of "UNC" in Tokyo in July 1950 and utilized about 200 U.S. military bases (now about 100) in Okinawa and mainland Japan as logistics bases for waging the U.S. war in Korea. Japan also became a launching pad for the U.S. air and naval attacks against the North Korean troops and facilities in Korea. For instance, two of the three Air Force groups within the U.S. Far East Air Forces (FEAF) were operating from Japan: the 5th Air Force at Nagoya and 20th Air Force at Kadena Air Base in Okinawa. In June 1950, FEAF had "a total of1,172 aircraft, including 365 F-80Cs."[8]

These fighter planes or bombers were flying from various air bases in Japan, including Itazuke, Yokota, Misawa, Kadena, etc. On July 16, "forty-seven aircraft from Kadena attacked the Seoul railway marshalling yards," and "by mid-August, ninety-eight B-29s were flying missions" from Yokota and Kadena Air Bases.[9] However, the Yoshida cabinet "did not acknowledge the nation's role in the war, and the people were unaware of it."[10]

The full extent of Japan's role in the Korean War is still difficult to assess since such history has been kept in secret to a large extent by both Governments of Japan and the U.S. As for the Japanese nationals who participated in the Korean War, the estimated number so far is at least 5,000, based on the public information available. They can be divided into three groups.

First, the "UNC" mobilized "3,922 Japanese LR (labor requisition) workers" who had manned some of the ships involved in the Operation Chromite

---

[8] Wada, pp.91-92
[9] *Ibid.*, p.92
[10] *Ibid.*, p.95

(amphibious landing of troops at Inchon) in September 1950.[11] These Japanese crews transported "79 percent of the U.S. Marine landing force" by steering "thirty-seven" LSTs (landing ship tanks) to the shore.[12]

The second group consisted of "1200" Japanese government employees of the Maritime Safety Board (MSB), including "fifty-four former Imperial Navy officers." Under MacArthur's order, the Japanese government provided a "total of fifty-four minesweepers" to assist the U.S. 7th Fleet, in the fall of 1950, for mine clearance operations at various harbors in Korea. The operation started at "Wonsan area on October 10" to clear the water for the U.S. military landing there. Other operations were carried out at "Inchon, Kunsan, Haeju, and Chinnampo."[13]

The third group consisted of "some 120" Japanese support workers who worked at the U.S. military bases in Japan and followed the U.S. soldiers to the Korean War zone in 1950. Included in this group were cooks, drivers, interpreters, maintenance workers, and teenagers who were kept by American soldiers as a "houseboy." Although small in number, they became part of the American military units in Korea by wearing the U.S. military uniforms, carrying guns, and fighting with the U.S. soldiers against the North Korean or Chinese troops on occasions. Some of them apparently died in the fighting, and the survivors were repatriated to Japan by the U.S. military by "middle of 1952," except "one of the two Japanese prisoners-of-war in North Korea arrived home in August 1953."[14]

Many Japanese died in the first six months of the War: "According to an estimate by Japan's Special Procurement Agency, 56 Japanese

---

[11] Tessa Morris-Suzuki, "Post-War Warriors: Japanese Combatants in the Korean War," *The Asia-Pacific Journal*, Vol. 10, Issue 31, No. 1, July 30, 2012
[12] Wada, p.113
[13] Wada, pp.138-139
[14] Moris-Suzuki, *ibid*.

sailors and laborers were killed," and "23 of the deaths occurred when Japanese-crewed ships were sunk by mines."**15**

3. Creation of Bogus "UN-GOJ SOFA" and "UNC" Logistic Bases

When the Treaty of Peace with Japan was signed on September 8, 1951, the U.S. Secretary of State Dean Acheson obtained from Prime Minister Yoshida of Japan the following commitment in an exchange of notes:

> "…If and when the forces of a member or members of the United Nations are engaged in any <u>United Nations action in the Far East</u> after the Treaty of Peace comes into force, Japan will permit and facilitate the support in and about Japan, by the member or members, of the forces engaged in such <u>United Nations action</u>…"**16** (Underline added)

Based on the notes, the USG subsequently obtained a more detailed agreement on the legal status and privileges of the soldiers and their dependents of the "United Nations forces" which were staying in or moving through Japan, in regard to the "United Nations action in Korea." Thus, on February 19, 1954, the Government of Japan (GOJ) signed the "Agreement Regarding the Status of the United Nations Forces in Japan" with the USG, acting as the Unified Command, and eight "Sending States."**17** Although no official of the United Nations signed this treaty, the "UNC" refers this agreement as the "UN-GOJ SOFA (Status of Forces Agreement)," pretending as if this agreement was made between the UN and Japan.**18**

---

15 Morris-Suzuki, *ibid*.
16 TIAS 2490
17 TIAS 2995
18 *See* United Nations Command-Rear Fact Sheet,
https://www.yokota.af.mil/Portals/44/Documents/Units/AFD-150924-004.pdf

Another serious U.S. misrepresentation in this Treaty is in the use of the term, "United Nations forces." Article I of the Treaty defines it as "those forces of the land, sea or air armed services of the <u>sending States which are sent to engage in action pursuant to the United Nations Resolutions.</u>"(Underline added) How did the armed forces of the "sending States" become "United Nations forces"? If the SC decided to assemble the armed forces from Members of the UN, in accordance with Article 42 and 43 of the UN Charter, such forces may be, indeed, called UN Forces, but that was not the case for the foreign armed forces sent to Korea in 1950. As pointed out previously, the UN's Office of Legal Affairs clarified in 1994 that the foreign forces sent to Korea was "similar to the allied military coalition set up in the Gulf War." The proper name for the coalition forces used to expel the Iraqi troops from Kuwait in the 1991 Gulf War was "U.S.-led Coalition Forces" or "U.S.-led Multinational Forces" in the case of U.S. invasion and occupation of Iraq in 2003.

Although the U.S. obtained a SC authorization for the coalition military operation in the Gulf War, President George H.W. Bush, to his credit, did not dare to repeat Truman's lies about the U.S.-led coalition forces in Korea as "UN Forces." In both Korean and Gulf Wars, the U.S.-led coalition forces were not under the command and control of the UN SC.

Aside from obtaining special privileges for the U.S.-led coalition forces staying or passing through Japan, it seems there were two real purposes for the "UN-GOJ SOFA": First, it was intended to secure a long-term, free use of certain U.S. bases in Japan as "UNC" logistics bases-even after the active fighting in Korea was halted with a cease-fire agreement in July 1953; Second, it was intended to provide an option, under Article 22, for the "UNC" to increase its coalition forces in Korea or Japan, if needed, in the future by allowing "any State not signatory to this Agreement" to join this Treaty any time, if such a State is willing to send its forces to the Far East in support of the "UN SC Resolutions of June 25, June 27 and July 7, 1950 and the UN GA Resolution of February 1, 1951."

Under Articles 24 and 25, this Treaty states that it "shall terminate" when "all the United Nations forces have been withdrawn from Japan" or within 90 days after the same forces "have been withdrawn from Korea." Does this mean this Treaty will continue to function indefinitely if the "UNC" keeps only one non-U.S. "UNC"soldier in Japan? The answer seems to be yes, in view of the current practice of the "UNC-Rear" office at Yokota Air Base. In 2018, there were only four "UNC" soldiers present at the "UNC-Rear" office, located at Yokota Air Base, with an Australian Air Force officer as the Commander and a Canadian Air Force officer as the Deputy Commander. Aside from Yokota, six other U.S. bases in Japan are also designated by USG and GOJ as the "UNC" bases: Camp Zama, Yokosuka Naval Base, Sasebo Naval Base, Kaneda Air Base, White Beach Naval Facility, and Futenma Marine Corps Air Station.

By imposing the fictitious "UN-GOJ SOFA" on Japan, the U.S.-led "UNC" again violated Article 9 of Japan's Peace Constitution by increasing the likelihood of Japan's involvement in another horrible war and making it impossible for the Japanese people to live in "peace for all time," as long as the Korean War continues on, and the "UNC-Rear" bases remain in Japan. If the War resumes in Korea again in the future, it is quite predictable that the USG will try to incorporate Japan's Self-Defense Forces into the "UNC" forces too to fight against the North Korea.

V Dissolution of "UNC" Is Long Overdue

1. UN Already Called for Dissolution of "UNC"

1975 marked a historic turning point in the UN General Assembly's discussion on the "Question of Korea," which had been going on there from 1947. As new nations joined the UN, after achieving their independence from the colonial powers in the post-WW II period, there was a growing support within the United Nations for self-determination of the Korean people and peaceful reunification of the divided Korea, without any foreign interference. This positive trend resulted at last in the invitation of the representatives of both Governments of Korea to participate in the GA discussion on the "Question of Korea" in 1975. After a heated debate, the GA, in a rather confusing way, adopted two different resolutions on Korea: Resolution 3390(xxx) A was based on a draft co-sponsored by the U.S. and its 27 allies, while Resolution 3390(xxx) B was based on a draft co-sponsored by the 43 non-aligned and socialist countries, including Algeria and the Peoples' Republic of China.

Interestingly, both Resolutions had a basic consensus that it was now necessary to dissolve the "United Nations Command" and withdraw all foreign troops serving under the UN flag in South Korea. However, the U.S.-sponsored Resolution attached a condition to the dissolution of the UNC: that "the parties directly concerned" should start talks and "new arrangements" be made for the "maintenance of the Armistice Agreement." On the other hand, Resolution B had no such condition and just called upon the "real parties to the Armistice Agreement" to replace the Korean Military Armistice Agreement with "a peace agreement." (Ref. 12)

In particular, it is to be noted that Resolution B used quotation marks on the term "United Nations Command" to express disapproval of such name for the first time in a UN resolution. (Ref. 12, A/RES/3390(XXX), November 18, 1975)

To a large extent, the adoption of Resolution B was a stunning victory for the DPRK and its supporters in the GA since Resolution B had more co-sponsors and more favorable voting result: 54(Yes)-43(No)-42(Abstention). In other words, more than two thirds of the voting Members supported Resolution B, if the votes for Abstention were added to the Yes votes. Those who were abstaining in the voting were probably leaning in support of the Resolution B but were reluctant to express it openly due to their fear of the USG. It is also to be noted that even some of the nations that sent troops to fight in Korea either supported Resolution B (Ethiopia) or abstained (Greece, Philippines and Thailand).

Unfortunately, no talks were held between the U.S., DPRK, ROK, and China to follow up on the two Resolutions. After the First Committee adopted Resolution B, the DPRK Government issued a statement,[1] expressing its willingness "to conclude a peace agreement with the United States…on the condition that all the foreign troops are withdrawn" from South Korea. On the other hand, USG was only interested in talks to assign the duties of the "UNC" in the Armistice Agreement to the U.S. and ROK militaries so that the U.S. troops could remain in South Korea. USG was also not willing to discuss a peace agreement at the time, without the participation of ROK government. On

---

[1] A/10354

apartheid, which remain the main obstacles to the strengthening of international peace and security,

Reaffirming the close link existing between the strengthening of international security, disarmament, decolonization, development and the need for a more intensive international effort to narrow the widening gap between the developed and the developing countries, and also stressing, in this connexion, the importance of the early implementation of the decisions adopted at its seventh special session,

Emphasizing the need constantly to strengthen the peace-keeping and peace-making role of the United Nations, as well as its role in promoting development through co-operation,

1. *Solemnly calls upon* all States to seek strict and consistent implementation of the purposes and principles of the Charter of the United Nations and of all the provisions of the Declaration on the Strengthening of International Security as a basis for relations among States, irrespective of their size, level of development and socio-economic system;

2. *Also calls upon* all States to extend the process of détente to all regions of the world, with the equal participation of all States, in order to bring about just and lasting solutions to international problems so that peace and security will be based on effective respect for the sovereignty and independence of all States and the inalienable rights of each people to determine its own destiny freely and without outside interference, coercion or pressure;

3. *Reaffirms* the legitimacy of the struggle of peoples under alien domination to achieve self-determination and independence and appeals to all States to implement the Declaration on the Granting of Independence to Colonial Countries and Peoples[11] and the other resolutions of the United Nations on the total elimination of colonialism, racism and *apartheid*;

4. *Reaffirms* that any measure or pressure directed against any State while exercising its sovereign right freely to dispose of its natural resources constitutes a flagrant violation of the right of self-determination of peoples and the principle of non-intervention, as set forth in the Charter, which, if pursued, could constitute a threat to international peace and security;

5. *Reaffirms* its opposition to any threats of use of force, intervention, aggression, foreign occupation and measures of political and economic coercion which attempt to violate the sovereignty, territorial integrity, independence and security of States;

6. *Recommends* urgent measures to stop the arms race and promote disarmament, including the convening of the World Disarmament Conference, the dismantling of foreign military bases, the creation of zones of peace and the encouragement of general and complete disarmament and strengthening of the United Nations, in order to eliminate the causes of international tensions and ensure international peace, security and co-operation;

7. *Takes note* of the report of the Secretary-General,[12] requests him to submit to the General Assembly at its thirty-first session a report on the implementation of the Declaration on the Strengthening of International Security and decides to include in the provisional agenda of its thirty-first session the item entitled "Implementation of the Declaration on the Strengthening of International Security".

2409th plenary meeting
18 November 1975

3390 (XXX). Question of Korea

A

The General Assembly,

Mindful of the hope expressed by it in resolution 3333 (XXIX) of 17 December 1974,

Desiring that progress be made towards the attainment of the goal of peaceful reunification of Korea on the basis of the freely expressed will of the Korean people,

Recalling its satisfaction with the issuance of the joint communiqué at Seoul and Pyongyang on 4 July 1972 and the declared intention of both the South and the North of Korea to continue the dialogue between them,

Further recalling that, by its resolution 711 A (VII) of 28 August 1953, the General Assembly noted with approval the Armistice Agreement of 27 July 1953,[13] and that, in its resolution 811 (IX) of 11 December 1954, it expressly took note of the provision of the Armistice Agreement which requires that the Agreement shall remain in effect until expressly superseded either by mutually acceptable amendments and additions or by provisions in an appropriate agreement for a peaceful settlement at a political level between both sides,

Aware, however, that tension in Korea has not been totally eliminated and that the Armistice Agreement remains indispensable to the maintenance of peace and security in the area,

Noting the letter of 27 June 1975,[14] addressed to the President of the Security Council by the Government of the United States of America, affirming that it is prepared to terminate the United Nations Command on 1 January 1976, provided that the other parties directly concerned reach agreement on alternative arrangements mutually acceptable to them for maintaining the Armistice Agreement,

Noting the statement of 27 June 1975 by the Government of the Republic of Korea affirming its willingness to enter into arrangements for maintaining the Armistice Agreement,

Recognizing that, in accordance with the purposes and principles of the Charter of the United Nations regarding the maintenance of international peace and security, the United Nations has a continuing responsibility to ensure the attainment of this goal on the Korean peninsula,

1. *Reaffirms* the wishes of its members, as expressed in the consensus statement adopted by the General Assembly on 28 November 1973,[15] and urges both the South and the North of Korea to continue their dialogue to expedite the peaceful reunification of Korea;

---
[11] Resolution 1514 (XV).
[12] A/10205 and Add.1.
[13] See *Official Records of the Security Council, Eighth Year, Supplement for July, August and September 1953*, document S/3079; transmitted to the members of the General Assembly by a note of the Secretary-General (A/2451).
[14] *Ibid., Thirtieth Year, Supplement for April, May and June 1975*, document S/11737.
[15] *Official Records of the General Assembly, Twenty-eighth Session, Supplement No. 30* (A/9030), p. 24, item 41.

Ref. 12, A-RES-3390(XXX), 한국문제 1975.11.18

---

the other hand, the DPRK Government was unwilling to allow the ROK Government's participation in the negotiation of a peace agreement because the latter refused to sign the Military Armistice Agreement in 1953 and the ROK military forces were under the operational control of the U.S. military. Nevertheless, North Korea has been open to the participation of ROK Government in the peace talks since 1997, when it agreed to the Four-Party Talks for a peace treaty in Korea. Unfortunately, such talks have been unsuccessful, due to the U.S. refusal to withdraw its troops from South Korea, even after signing a peace treaty.

2. "UNC" Has Been a Hollow Outfit from 1978

After the Korean War Armistice Agreement was signed in 1953, the 16 foreign nations in the "UNC" started to withdraw their troops from South Korea, and most of the foreign troops returned to their home countries by early 1970s, except for the U.S. troops. In 1975, there were still some 40,000 U.S. troops in South Korea. However, a U.S. representative made a surprise announcement to the UN GA delegates in November 1975 that the "UNC" had "less than 300" American soldiers, and that the rest of the U.S. troops were stationed in South Korea under "a bilateral agreement."(Mutual Defense Treaty of 1953)

Along with the growing demand in the GA for the dissolution of the "UNC," USG proposed to create a new U.S.-ROK military structure that would still allow the U.S. military to continue its operational control over the ROK armed forces. Thus, a new military entity called the "ROK-US Combined Forces Command" (CFC) was established on November 7, 1978, with the Commander of "UNC" also commanding the CFC. At this time, the ROK Government delegated its "operational control of South Korean forces to the CFC." While the Korean forces "moved from UNC to CFC control, American forces did not follow." Instead, they were "placed under varying degrees of control under USFK."[2] However, in 1994, the South Korean Government took back its

---

2   Col. Shawn P. Creamer, U.S. Army, "The United Nations Command and The Sending States," *International Journal of Korean Studies*, Vol. XXI, No. 2, Fall-Winter 2017, p.14

peacetime operational control of the ROK forces from CFC. The main role of the CFC at present is to plan and control the ROK-U.S. combined war drills in peacetime; however, in case of hostilities, CFC claims that it will become a "war-fighting headquarters" with "operational control over more than 600,000 active-duty military personnel of all services, of both countries."[3]

With the CFC in place, the mission of "UNC" has been on maintaining Armistice in Korea, controlling the DMZ area, guarding the Panmunjom area, keeping its military bases in Japan, and planning for bringing in foreign troops into Korea again in case of a crisis in the future. In particular, it wants to retain its use of the seven "UNC-Rear" military bases in Japan, which is secured under the "UN-GOJ SOFA." As pointed out previously, there are only four "UNC" personnel at the "UNC-Rear" office in Japan at present. Moreover, the number of current military personnel in the "UNC" HQ at Camp Humphreys, Pyongtaek, appears to be about 40 according to a group picture shown on its website. Thus, the dissolution of "UNC" HQ and "UNC-Rear" HQ would have a minimum impact on the overall military stability in Korea at this time. Besides, such a step will not affect in any way the U.S. military presence in South Korea and Japan since the USG is claiming that they are stationed there under the bilateral mutual security agreements with the ROK and Japan.

3. Trying to Revive the Obsolete "UNC"

In the last ten years, the USG has been taking small steps to revive the moribund "UNC." In 2010, Australia agreed to provide one officer to command the "UNC-Rear" HQ. In 2011, Canada sent three officers to the "UNC" HQ and one officer to the "UNC-Rear" HQ. By 2014, USG

---

3 *See* USFK website, www.usfk.mil/about/combined-forces-command

decided to pursue "a more formal multinational staffing arrangement for augmenting the UNC HQ staff," In particular, the "UNC" enhanced the roles of the Assistant Chiefs of Staff for Operations (U-3) and Logistics (U-4), bolstering "the Multinational Coordination Center (MNCC) within the U-3" after 2015[4]

The main objective of this "revitalization" program seems to be to increase the capacity and preparedness of the "UNC" so that it could be used "for combat purposes" too in the future.[5] Another objective of this program seems to be to make the "UNC" look like a real international military operation. This effort took on a political dimension in January 2018, when the USG and the Canadian Government co-hosted the "Vancouver Foreign Ministers' Meeting on Security and Stability on the Korean Peninsula" in Canada. This Meeting was mainly a new initiative of the Trump administration to implement its "Maximum Pressure" strategy of enforcing sanctions against North Korea with the assistance of the Member States of the "UNC" plus several related countries. One notable presence in this Meeting was Japan's Foreign Minister. This is, perhaps, an indication that the USG may be pushing Japan to join the "UNC" as an official member in the future.)

Several months after the Vancouver Meeting, USG rewarded Canada by designating a Canadian Lt. General (Army) as the first, non-U.S. Deputy Commander of the "UNC." Then, in July 2019, USG appointed an Australian Vice Admiral (Navy) to become the next Deputy Commander of the "UNC". In addition, the "UNC" finally created its own website too[6] in 2020. In the past, its website was included in the USFK website. According to this new website, the "UNC" now consists

---

[4] Col. Shawn P. Creamer, pp.17-19
[5] "S. Korea Peace Drive Complicated by 'Revitalization' of UN Command," *Financial Times*, Oct. 2, 2018

of "Australia, Belgium, Canada, Columbia, Denmark, France, Greece, Italy, Netherlands, New Zealand, Norway, the Philippines, Republic of South Africa, Thailand, Turkey, the United Kingdom, the United States, and the Republic of Korea, as the host nation." This list indicates that there was a change in the membership of the "UNC." In the beginning, its membership consisted of sixteen foreign nations that provided combat troops to the "UNC" plus the ROK. However, Luxembourg and Ethiopia withdrew from the "UNC" in 1953 and 1965 respectively; but Norway, Denmark and Italy joined the "UNC" in 1999, 2000 and 2013 respectively. It is not clear whether the three new Member States, which had provided medical aid for the wounded in the Korean War, made any commitment to provide any combat troops to the "UNC" in case of any renewed fighting in Korea.

Furthermore, it is also not clear at this time whether the old Member States of the "UNC" will be willing to provide any combat troops to

Vancouver "UNC" Sending States Foreign Ministers Meeting

---

6   www.unc.mil

the fake "UNC" entity again in the future. After all, a strong argument can be made that the original authority and mission provided in the SCR 83 and 84 in 1950 have expired already. In other words, if there is a new fighting in Korea in the future, the "UNC" will have no legal authority to wage the war again on its own. It will have to obtain a new authorization from the UN SC. This conclusion is supported by two legal experts who reviewed this issue: "Strong policy interests make it advisable that Security Council authorizations to use force be terminated by the establishment of a cease-fire unless explicitly and unambiguously continued by the Council itself."[7] Thus, it is reasonable to assume that, together with the armistice in 1953, Resolution 83 and 84 of the 1950 Security Council has expired.

4. Use of "UNC" to Continue the Endless Korean War

The USG's main argument for keeping the "UNC" alive in the past has been that the "UNC" is a party to the Korean Armistice Agreement(AA) and, therefore, it cannot be dissolved prior concluding "alternative arrangements for the maintenance of the Armistice Agreement" are made.[8] But there are a few problems with this logic. First, did the U.S. have the legal authority to sign the Armistice Agreement in the name of the "UNC"? The answer is no since SCR 84 never authorized USG the use of "UNC" name. Thus, the Agreement itself was illegal and void for failing to meet basic requirements of a legal contract. Second, if the U.S. was serious in finding an alternative arrangement for maintaining the AA, then why did it not propose to the DPRK that it would return

---

[7] Jules Lobel and Michael Ratner, "Bypassing the Security Council: Ambiguous Authorizations to Use Force, Cease-Fires and the Iraqi Inspection Regime," *The American Journal of International Law*, Jan. 1999; Vol. 93, pp.144-145.

[8] *See* A/RES/3390 (XXX) A, 1975

its operational control of the South Korean armed forces to the ROK Government and also transfer the duties of the "UNC" to the ROK military? Finally, who is blocking the alternative arrangements to the Armistice Agreement? It is to be noted that the DPRK Government had proposed a peace treaty to the USG from 1974, and participated in the Four-Party Peace Talks (ROK, DPRK, U.S., and China) in 1997-1999. The two Koreas also joined the UN as a Member in 1991 and signed a historic Non-Aggression Agreement, including the establishment of a "South-North Military Committee." In addition, the two leaders of Korea held three Korean Summits in 2018 and they signed a comprehensive military agreement on September 19, 2018. This latest agreement also included a pledge to establish an Inter-Korean Joint Military Committee.

Unfortunately, these two military agreements between the South and North Korea could not be implemented fully due to the USG's objections and its continuing operational control over the South Korean military forces. For instance, former U.S. Secretary of State Mike Pompeo expressed his "discontent" to the ROK Foreign Minister Kang in September 2018, regarding the South-North Military Agreement.[9] In short, the Korean leaders cannot implement any alternative military agreement to replace the outdated, broken Korean Armistice Agreement of 1953 or sign a South-North peace agreement, as long as the USG continues to hold on its wartime operational control over the ROK military forces. Thus, the USG's excuse of keeping the "UNC" for the purpose of maintaining the Armistice Agreement is bogus. Besides, the U.S.-led "UNC" has been the most serious violator of the Armistice Agreement, including bringing in tactical U.S. nuclear weapons into South Korea in 1958.

---

[9] *Reuters*, Oct. 18, 2018

In fact, it is likely that the USG prefers to keep the current Armistice system over a permanent peace on the Korean Peninsula. There are several unspoken reasons why the USG has refused to sign a peace treaty to end the costly Korean War. They are 1) to retain overall control over the DMZ area, including all inter-Korean exchanges and economic activities, in the name of the "UNC"; 2) to keep the state of war in Korea so that the U.S. military companies can sell more expensive weapons to South Korea; and 3) to keep the U.S. bases and troops in Korea. According to a U.S. military directive in 1983, the Commander of the "UNC" is tasked, in case hostilities are resumed in Korea, to "employ UNC forces, maintain UNC and CFC as separate legal and military entities."[10] However, it seems it will be inevitable that the U.S. military commander, as the Commander-in-Chief of the "UNC," will ultimately command all foreign and ROK forces, even if the US military returns its wartime operational control of the South Korean military to the ROK Government in the future.

---

[10] *See* "US CJCS Terms of Reference for Commander UNC," January 19, 1983

VI Conclusion

Abraham Lincoln is famous for his profound, moving speeches. One of them is about lies: "You can fool all the people some of the time and some of the people all the time, but you cannot fool all the people all the time." His words of wisdom sound so true, as we uncover the elaborate lies upon which the magnificent edifice of the "UNC" was built up in the early period of the Korean War. We hope this pamphlet has shined some light on the lingering myth of the "UNC" as an agency of the UN.

At a time when the USG is trying to revive the moribund "UNC," it is all the more critical for the Korean people and the international community to understand the real identity of the "UNC" and its lies so that we would be no longer fooled by the Cold War warriors who want to keep the Korean War going and keep using the "UNC" to dominate Korea and Japan forever.

A summary of our findings and analysis on the fake "UNC" is as follows:

1) The UN Security Council did not establish the "UNC" on July 7, 1950. It merely "recommended" to Member States of the UN to make their forces available to a "Unified Command" under the United States.

2) The Truman administration created the "Unified Command" immediately upon the adoption of the SC Resolution 84. However, for political and propaganda purposes, USG established a new military

command called the "United Nations Command" in Tokyo on July 25, 1950. There has been much confusion about the two entities because the USG has used both names on different occasions as either one suited its purposes. The two names are like two faces of the same coin.

3) The USG, which was dominating the UN in 1950, abused the UN system and name in order to justify its military intervention in the Korean civil war as "a police action" of the UN, to depict the U.S.-led foreign forces as "UN Forces," to subjugate the South Korean military under the control of the U.S. military, and to induce Japan's cooperation in the Korean War.

4) The SC Resolutions 82, 83 and 84 in question were adopted quickly without a due process, in violation of many Articles of the UN Charter. They were illegal to a large extent. In addition, the USG often undermined the UN Charter by taking unilateral actions in Korea, even before any UN resolutions were taken, or by distorting the language or meaning of the words in the UN Charter or UN resolutions.

5) Although a U.S. general signed the Korean Armistice Agreement of 1953 in the name of "UNC," the UN was not a party to the Agreement because the "UNC" represented the USG interests only. In fact, it has been under the control of the USG only from the beginning of its birth. The legality of the Armistice Agreement itself is in much doubt.

6) The original mission of the Unified Command/"UNC" expired long time ago, when all the foreign troops, except the U.S. forces, left South Korea after the Armistice Agreement was signed in 1953; when the UN GA adopted a resolution for dissolution of "UNC" in 1975; when both South and North Korea joined the UN as a Member of the UN and signed a Non-Aggression Agreement in 1991; or when a comprehensive South-North military agreement for peace was signed in September 2018.

7) The Office of Legal Affairs of the United Nations issued a legal opinion in 1994, confirming that "the so-called 'United Nations Command' is a misnomer."

8) The US-led "UNC" has violated the sovereignty of Korea by subjugating the ROK military under its control, occupying Korean territories, and preventing inter-Korean cooperation for peace and development.

9) The "UNC" still presents a major obstacle to achieving a lasting peace, real independence, and peaceful reunification of Korea by the Korean people themselves, without foreign interferences.

10) Above all, the USG bears the heaviest legal responsibility, under the UN Charter, to terminate the fake "UNC" and the moribund Unified Command (USG), as soon as possible, because the two entities are under its control. In particular, Article 2(2) of the UN Charter requires that "all Members shall fulfill in good faith the obligations assumed by them in accordance with the present Charter." The basic obligation of a UN Member is to act in accordance with the purposes and principles of the United Nations, as specified in Article 1 and 2 of the UN Charter. In other words, the USG cannot continue to violate Korea's sovereignty or deny Korean people's basic human rights to self-determination, peace and development by abusing the UN name. It is hoped that the current U.S. administration would remember the old commitment made to the UN GA meeting in 1975 by then Secretary of State Henry Kissinger:

"The United States agrees that 20 years after the end of the Korean War it is timely to terminate the United Nations Command." Well, it is now almost 70 years later.

In addition, both Governments of Korea and Japan also bear significant responsibility to undertake all necessary actions to terminate the fake "UNC" in their land, including refusal to cooperate with the fake "UNC," asking it to leave their land, or taking legal actions against it.

Finally, it is also incumbent upon the people and civil society of the world to raise their voices to abolish the fake "UNC." In particular, the

civil society groups in Korea, the U.S. and Japan should work together to dissolve the fake "UNC" so that the endless, costly Korean War can be ended finally with a peace agreement. If you are a concerned group or individual who believes the termination of the fake "UNC" is long overdue, please sign our Declaration for Dissolution of the Fake "UN Command," which is posted in our website. Let's make sure that such termination will be carried out by the 70th anniversary of the Korean Armistice Agreement in 2023.

Abolish the Fake "UN Command"!
End the Endless Korean War now!

Appendix A

Declaration for Dissolution of the Fake "UN Command"

On July 7, 1950, the UN Security Council (SC) recommended, in its Resolution 84 (S/1588), the creation of a U.S.-led "Unified Command,"("UC") but the United States soon established another entity called the "United Nations Command" ("UNC"), in violation of the SC Resolution.

As it was clarified by the UN Secretary-General Boutros Boutros-Ghali in 1994, and confirmed again by the UN Under-Secretary-General Rosemary DiCarlo at a SC meeting in September 2018 that the so-called "UNC" is "not a UN Specialized Agency or Subsidiary organ nor does it come under the command and control of the UN."

Furthermore, SC Resolution 84 itself was adopted in violation of the UN Charter (without "concurring votes" of the USSR), the General Assembly Resolutions on UN emblem and flag, and the first UN Flag Code (December 19, 1947). In particular, the SC had no authority to authorize a non-UN entity, such as the UC, to use the UN flag in its military operations.

On November 18, 1975, the UN General Assembly (GA) took a bold step to stop the abuse of the UN name by adopting its Resolution A/RES/3390B, which stated that "it is necessary to dissolve the 'United Nations Command.'"

Moreover, the U.S. should have terminated the "UNC" long time ago in any case, since the main purpose of the SCR 84 had been achieved with the Korean military cease-fire agreement in 1953 and the withdrawal of all foreign troops, except the U.S., from Korea by the end of 1970s, and the subsequent entry of both Koreas (ROK and DPRK) into the United Nations as official Member States in 1991.

However, instead of dissolving the fake entity, the U.S. Government has been trying in recent years to revive the moribund "UNC" so that it could continue its endless war against North Korea, while forcing the ROK Government to buy billions of dollars of new U.S. weapons.

In addition, the U.S. quibbled about its jurisdiction over the southern part of the DMZ and expanded the mission of "UNC" in 2018, to block the inter-Korean development projects, such as connecting a network of the railroads and roads across the DMZ.

These reactionary moves are creating new obstacles against the strong aspirations of the Korean people to work for a lasting peace, reconciliation, cooperation, and development in Korea.

Thus, as concerned individuals or organizations, we sign this declaration calling for a prompt dissolution of the fake "UNC," in support of the Korean people's rights to peace and justice.

1. The so-called "UNC" is neither a subsidiary body nor an agency of the United Nations.
2. The U.S. should stop the illegal use of the UN flag by the "UNC."
3. The U.S. should stop abusing the name of the United Nations by promptly dissolving the U.S.-controlled "UNC" in Korea and "UNC-Rear" in Japan. 4. The U.S. should implement the 1975 UN GA resolution, calling for dissolution of the "United Nations Command" and replacement of the "Korean Military Armistice Agreement with a peace agreement."

5. The international community, including all UN Member States and civil society groups, has responsibility to refuse all cooperation with the fake "UNC" and work for an early termination of the misleading entity in order to protect the UN name and dignity.

6. An early termination of the fake "UNC" will also contribute to a full implementation of the inter-Korean summit agreements, an official ending of the endless Korean War, full exercise of self-determination by the Korean people, and the advancement of UN law as well as international law in the world.

October 12, 2021

(Endorse this Declaration by visiting www.fakeunc.org)

Appendix B — Steering Committee

Jang-Hie LEE (President for Citizen's Solidarity for Peace & unification) Chairperson

Kyungwan Ryu (Co-President of Korea International Peace Forum) Executive Director

Kwon, Oh-Hyouck (Secretary General)

John Kim, Attorney (U.S.)

Mee Il Lee (Director of Korea International Peace Forum)

KoEun, Kwang-Soon (President of the Peace Mothers of Korea)

Park, Young-tae (Director of Korea International Peace Forum)

Jean(Yeonjin) Chung (Co-President of Action One Korea)

Lee, Gi-Myo (Co-President of Action One Korea)

Lee, Si-woo (Photographer)

Kim, Jong-kwi (Chair of Lawyers for a Democratic Society Research Committee on USFK Affairs Peace Mothers of Korea)

Shin Ella (Director of Self-Unification / The Progressive Party)

Appendix C — Supporting Organizations and Individuals

1. Domestic Organizations and Individuals

<Academia>

Cho, Young-gun (Professor Emeritus OF Kyungnam University)

Jang-Hie LEE (Professor Emeritus, Hankuk University of Foreign Studues)

Yim, hun young (The Center for Historical Truth and Justice)

Lee, Jae-Bong (Professor of Political Science at Wonkwang University)

Lee, Rea Kyoung (The Tomorrow)

Choi, Young-Ki (Professor Emeritus, Changwon national University)

<expert>

Lee Si-woo (Photographer)

<Law Group and Lawyer>

Lawyers for a Democratic Society Research Committee on USFK Affairs (ROK)

Park, Jinseok (Lawyer)

Shim, Jaewhan (Lawyer)

Kim, Jongkwi (Lawyer)

Heo, Jinsun (Lawyer)

Kweon, Jungho (Lawyer)

Nam, Sungwook (Lawyer)

Park, Samsung (Lawyer)

Oh, Minae (Lawyer)

<Social Group>

KoEun, Kwang-Soon (Peace Mothers of Korea)

Ye, In Chul / Han, Sung / An, Seng Moon (People's Congress for Korea Peace Federation)

Lee, Gi Myo / Hong Geun Jin / Jean(Yeonjin) Chung (Action One Korea)

Yun, Gi Jean (Solidarity for People's Sovereignty)

Lee, Yang Soo (Democratic Workers' National Conference)

Han, Chan-wook (Secretary general of April Revolution Society)

Lee, Yun (External Relations Chairperson of April Revolution Society)

Park, Haeng-Deuk (National Federation of Peasant Society)

Chang, Nam-Su (National Democratic Movement Families Association)

Kim, Ok Im (Korean Women' Peasant Association)

Han, Mi Kyung (National Women's Solidarity)

LEE, Gyu-Jae (National Unification National Unity South Korea Headquarters)

Kwak, Ho-Nam (Progressive College Student Network)

Kwon, Rak Gi (Unification Square)

Kwon, Oh Heon (Support Committee for Prisoners of Conscience for Justice, Peace and Human Rights)

Han, Chung Mog (Korea Progressive Solidarity)

Kim, Soo Nam (Our National Federation of Unification Promotion)

Kim, Jin Soo (National Poverty Alliance)

Kyungwan Ryu (Korea International Peace Forum)

Choi, Young-chan (Poverty Reduction Practice Solidarity)
Ch,o Duck-deok (Democratization Practice Family Movement Council)
Kim, Myung Hwan (Korean Confederation of Trade Unions)
Lee, Jang-Hie / HONG, Seong Mi / Shim, Jong Sook / LEE Changho / Shin Soo Seek (Citizen's Solidarity for Peace & Unification)
Kim, gi jun / Lee, cheon-dong (The Korea Veterans for Peace)
Chi, chul (Sovereign Broadcasting Ceo)
Kim, Bong Jun/Lee, daesoo(Eurasia Peace Way)

<Individuals>
Nam, Ki Bang (Daejeon Sejong Construction Branch)
Imsik Yoon
Jinyoung Lee

<party>
Lee, Sang-gyu (Jinbo-Party)
Former Rep. Kim, Jong-hoon
Soohwan Jung (Jinbo-Party Gwangju City)
Kweon, Eui seok (Jinbo-Party Daejeon City Chapter)

2. International organization

<International Association of Democratic Lawyers - IADL>
Jeanne Mirer (President IADL)
Bennamani Yasmine (Algeria Lawyer)
Mario (Haiti Lawyer)
Edre U. Olialia (Philippine Lawyer, National Union of People's Lawyers)
A.B.Lashari (Pakistan Lawyer)
Mahammad Masaud Ghani (Pakistan Lawyer)
Niloper (Indian Lawyer)

<Confederation of Lawyers of Asia and the Pacific-COLAP(Japan)>
Jun Sasamoto (Japanese Lawyer, COLAP Secretary General)
Hasan Abraar (Pakistan Lawyer, COLAP Vice President)

<Peace Women Partners International (Asia)>

3. Foreign Organization and Individuals

Canada
Michel Chossudovsky (Professor Emeritus, University of Ottawa, President and Director of The Centre for Research on Globalization)
Tamara Lorincz (Ontario, Canada, National Board of The Canadian Voice of Women for Peace)
Peace Philosophy Centre, Vancouver

Bangladesh
Policy Research for Development Alternative

Japan
Fujii Katsuhiko (Japan Nagoya, War Against Network)
Ishii Hiroshi (Japan Tokyo, Employee)
Isogai Jiro(Japan Aichi, Author)
Jung Jong Soon (Japan Nagoya, Care Worker)
Sakai Kenji (Japan Nagoya, War Against Network)
Yamamoto Mihagi (Japan Nagoya, Group Staff)

Ozawa Takashi (Japan Tokyo, Japan-Korea People's Solidarity National Network)

Watanabe Kenju (Japan Tokyo, Japan-Korea People's Solidarity National Network)

Kitagawa Hirokazu (Japan Saitama, 'Japan-Korea Analysis' Editor)

Kato Masaki (Japan Tokyo, Japan-Korea People's Solidarity National Network)

Japan-Korea People's Solidarity National Network

Japan's Committee for Independent Peaceful Unification of Korea

Kimura Hideto (Japan Nagasaki, Association to Protect Human Rights of Koreans in Nagasaki)

Park Sukyung (Japan Nagasaki)

Funakawa Shunichiro (Japan Saga)

Ogata Takaho (Japan Fukuoka)

Ito Kanji (Japan Fukuoka)

Someki Tomiyo (Japan Nagasaki)

Kanesaki Akira (Japan Fukuoka)

Ishikawa Akiko (Japan Fukuoka)

Hamaguchi Mariko (Japan Fukuoka)

Kuwano Yasuo (Japan Yamaguchi, Shimonoseki, Which Links Japan and Korea)

Abe Fukuyoshi (Japan Fukuoka)

Mizuguchi Yoko (Japan Fukuoka)

Tsuboi Hideo (Japan Oita)

Mizuguchi Tunemitu (Japan Fukuoka)

Kajiwara Tokusaburo (Japan Oita)

Santo Tadayoshi (Japan Fukuoka)

Kashiwagi Teruyoshi (Japan Fukuoka)

Suenaga Toshikazu (Japan Fukuoka)

Miguchi Motomu (Japan Fukuoka)

Matsuzaki Hiromi (Japan Fukuoka)

Motumura Makoto (Japan Fukuoka)

Suenaga Hiromi (Japan Fukuoka)

Urahata Kazuhisa (Japan Oita)

Sanmaru Shoko (Japan Oita)

Kurokawa Toshie (Japan Fukuoka)

Nakagawa Masami (Japan Fukuoka)

Inaba Setsuko (Japan Fukuoka)

Haga Akio (Japan Fukuoka)

Murata Kazuko (Japan Fukuoka)

Watanabe Hiroko (Japan Fukuoka)

Suzuki Masaaki (Japan Fukuoka)

Furukawa Natsukazu (Japan Fukuoka)

Tashiro Masami (Japan Nagasaki)

Sugauchi Takao (Japan Fukuoka)

Ono Yasunori (Japan Fukuoka)

Hosoi Akemi (Japan Tokyo, Meeting of citizen's opinion 30-Tokyo)

Members of Japan-Korea "Stonewalk Korea"

Japan International Lawyers Association

Sweden

Agneta Norberg (Hägersten, Stockholm, Sweden, chair Swedish Peace Council, and a board member of Directors for Global Network Against Weapons and Nuclear Power in Space.)

Swedish Peace Council

America

Citizens Opposing Active Sonar Threats (U.S.)

Global Network against Weapons and Nuclear Power in Space (U.S.)

Indong Oh (Co-Chair, June 15 U.S. Committee for Korea Reunification)

U.S. Support Committee for Korean Prisoners of Conscience / Kim, Shiwhan / Song, Young / Wang, Yongeun

Minjung Solidarity of New York / Han, Iksoo

Pan- Korean Alliance for Reunification in USA / Paik, Seung Bae

Korean American National Coordinating Council / Kim, Hyun Hwan

Korean Peace Alliance / Ha, Yong Jin

World Beyond War (U.S.)

Alice Slater (NY, USA, World Beyond War)

Amy Harlib (NY, USA, Yoga For Peace, Justice, Harmony With the Planet)

Ariel Ky (Oceanside, CA, USA, a peace visionary)

Bob Reynolds

Bruce Gagnon (ME, USA, Global Network against Weapons and Nuclear Power in Space)

Russell Wray (Hancock, ME, USA, Citizens Opposing Active Sonar Threats (COAST)

Natasha Mayers, (ME, USA, Union of Maine Visual Artists)

William Griffin (Philadelphia, PA, USA, The Peace Report (Media Organization For Peace)

Carol Urner (Oregon, US, U.S. Women's International League for Peace and Freedom)

Charles Ryu (Paul's United Methodist Church)

Christopher Helali (Dartmouth College)

chris edstrom

David Gainesville

Dennis Apel (CA, USA, Catholic Worker)

Des Moines Catholic Worker (U.S.)

Diana Bohn (CA, USA, Member of the City of Berkeley Peace and Justice Commission)

Donald Han

Erdman Palmore

Frank Cordaro (IA, USA, Catholic Worker)

frank scott

Environmentalists against War (U.S.)

Janet Weil (Veterans for Peace)

John Kesich

John Steinmeyer (Veterns for Peace)

Kathleen Williams

Linval DePass

Larry Egly

Marc Cryer

Moon Jang (People's Party in NY)

Mr.Gulfport

Melissa Fleming

Holly Graham (USA, performer)

Ji-Yeon Yuh (Korea Policy Institute)

Koohan Paik Mander (Hawaii, USA)

Linda Novenski (Veterans for Peace)

National Association of Korean Americans (U.S.)

Patricia Heather-Lea

Ramsay Liem (MA, USA, Emeritus professor, Boston College)

Channing and Popai Llem Education Foundation Brookline

Peace Action Maine (U.S.)

Peaceworkers (U.S.)

Popai Liem Education Foundation (U.S.)

Presbyterian Peace Network for Korea (U.S.)

Prof. Subrata Ghoshroy (Cambridge, MA, USA, Visiting Professor Tokyo Institute of Technology and Research Affiliate Program in Science, Technology, and Society and Massachusetts Institute of Technology)

Rev. Kil Sang Yoon Korean-American

Sally-Alice Thompson

Steve Livingston (hicago Anti-War Coalition)

Soobok Kim (615 American Committee, N.Y.)

St. Columban Mission Society (U.S.)

Veterans For Peace-Korea Peace Campaign (U.S.)

Washington Fellowship of Reconciliation (U.S.)

William Sweet

England

Angie Zelter (Knighton Powys, Shropshire, UK, candidate for the 2012 Nobel Peace Prize and founder of Trident Ploughshares)

Dave Webb (Leeds, West Yorkshire, UK, Chair of the UK Campaign for Nuclear Disarmament and Convenor of the Global Network against Weapons and Nuclear Power in Space, Vice President of the International Peace Bureau.)

Lindis Percy, (Harrogate, North Yorkshire, UK, Co Founder of the Campaign for the Accountability of American Bases - (CAAB)

Trident Ploughshares, XR Peace

India

Aruna Kammila (Visakhapatnam, India, Assistant Professor at Damodaram Sanjivayya National Law University)

Baburao Kammila (Visakhapatnam, India)

Sai Harnath Abhilash Dhulipudi, (Bangalore, Karnataka, India)

Venkata Akhilesh Dhulipdi(Bangalore, Karnataka, India)

Jammu Narayana Rao (India, Director, Global Network Against Weapons and Nuclear Power in Space)

Australia

Marrickville Peace Group (NSW, Australia)

Nick Deane (NSW, Australia, Convenor of the Marrickville Peace Group)

AABCC / Australian Anti-Bases Campaign Coalition

Denis Doherty (Sydney Australia, AABCC national co-ordinator)

Dr. Hannah Middleton (Sydney Australia, Stop Star Wars campaigner for AABCC)

Sherrin Hibbard (Palmerston Island, Cook Islands, Australia, Principal, Palmerston Lucky School)

Germany

Paul Schneiss (Heidelberg, Germany)

6.15 National Committee-Europe (Germany)

International Network of Engineers and Scientists for Global Responsibility